Working in a Battlefield

Wai Chun Chiang

Copyright © 2014 **Wai Chun Chiang**
All rights reserved.

ISBN: **1499220243**
ISBN 13: **978-1499220247**

For My Family

Forward

This book analyzes a number of phenomena in the workplace that do not exist under perfect competition. When labor is not priced in accordance with productivity, be it due to measurement cost or imperfect information, the worker tends to shirk so that his actual productivity would be smaller than his potential productivity. Although being fired is possible, the worker knows also that this threat may not be genuine because it may be more profitable not to fire the worker if the worker produces an output level that lowers the average fixed cost by a sufficient extent.

An interesting angle offered in this book is that, if economic rent exists when every worker delivers his full productivity, this potential economic rent motivates the company to find ways to keep up the actual productivity; at the same time it also indicates the degree to which the employees can shirk such that the company still continues its business. This angle effectively treats the degree of "rent dissipation" as an interior-solution equilibrium.

To some extent, the employer can reduce shirking by institutionalizing certain incentive schemes, such as promotion, best-employee award, etc. On the other hand, the employer may attempt to overcome the asymmetric-information problem through probation arrangement, hiring a team manager who has a better idea of the productivity of each worker in the team, etc. However the workers may not react to the incentive schemes in a positive way when such schemes are based on relative performance rather than absolute productivity, because making other workers perform worse can be an alternative.

This book also points out that even if firing is a real threat to certain workers, taking into account the employer's fixed-cost consideration, the workers may counter by forming a union to enhance their bargaining position. As a result, rent dissipation and shirking – actual performance being lower than potential performance – are equilibrium.

Let me describe an echoing observation as the end of this forward. It is rather common that restaurants are not owned by the chef. The owner employs the chef not only as a cook but also as the team manager of the chef's crew. The chef surely is better informed about the actual and potential productivities of the members in his crew than the restaurant owner because they usually are the chef's apprentices. And, interestingly, the chef and the apprentices usually join or resign together. Remaining as a team could be the long run equilibrium for them, as this minimizes the asymmetric-information problem and rent dissipation.

Choi, Ka Fai

Table of Contents:

Introduction

Chapter 1: Concept of Potential Performance Curve

Chapter 2: More Concepts for PPC

Chapter 3: Considering Selfishness

Chapter 4: How Do Employers Deal with PPC? & Push Up the APC

Chapter 5: Paradox of Exploitation

Chapter 6: Unions

Conclusion

Introduction

Working in a Battlefield

Don't you think the workplace is a battlefield? You are in a battle with your friends and enemies, some of your colleagues, and your boss every day. They can be your friends on one day and your killer on the next day. How can we survive in this cold-blooded society in a logically, easier way? And why do we have to live like this? Is there any other choice?

Battlefield?

How is the amount of your paycheck determined? Most bosses may say that it is based on your performance. That is basically true. Therefore, most of your colleagues will try their hardest to "show" their best performance to claim their best return. I use the word "show" here because people may not have good performance in their work all the time, but they can still have the best performance in the group by making you look bad. That is "killing" in the workplace. Killing others so that you can survive is called a battle. The workplace is, no doubt, a battlefield.

Chapter 1

Concept of Potential Performance Curve

Equal Wage

There is a new fast-food restaurant that just opened on the corner of the street with five of the same job opportunities available, for example. After a period of job interviews, the boss decides to hire these five people: John, David, Mary, Peter, and Sue. Since they all are newly hired employees, the boss is not familiar with their work performance. They will all receive the same wage of $5.00 an hour. As we know, different people have different talents. Someone can do a job well, but some others cannot. Now I assume these five employees' potential wages based on performance on the same job are as follows:

John	$10/hour
David	$7/hour
Mary	$9/hour
Peter	$8/hour
Sue	$6/hour

What is potential performance? It is the maximum return from a person. Here it implies that the person cannot produce any more than the maximum return when other factors remain unchanged.

Now I rank these five employees by their potential performance as follows:

John	$10/hour
Mary	$9/hour
Peter	$8/hour
David	$7/hour
Sue	$6/hour

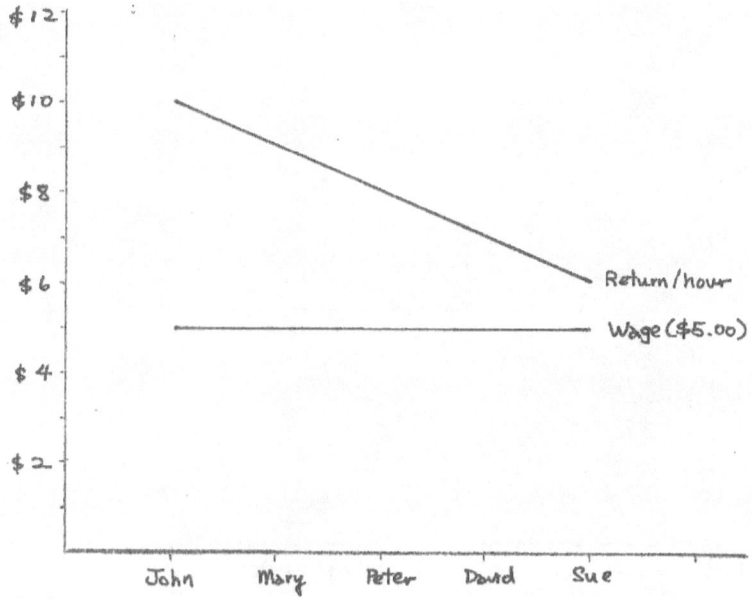

Fig.1. 1

If all employees are doing their best without considering any selfishness, the total return per hour will be $40 ($10+$9+$8+$7+$6), and the total cost per hour for hiring employees will be $25 ($5 x 5). The total gain per hour for hiring these five employees will be $15 ($40 - $25). Here we assume there is no fixed expense such as rent. In this case, all employees can have their stable wage, $5 per hour, and the boss can have a profit of $15 per hour. See figure 1.1.

It is not really necessary to rank the employees, in fact. However, it will look better and make it easier to compare the potential performance of each employee, indeed. You will see that the ranked chart will be very useful in later sections in this book. If we don't rank the employees, the chart will look like figure 1.2.

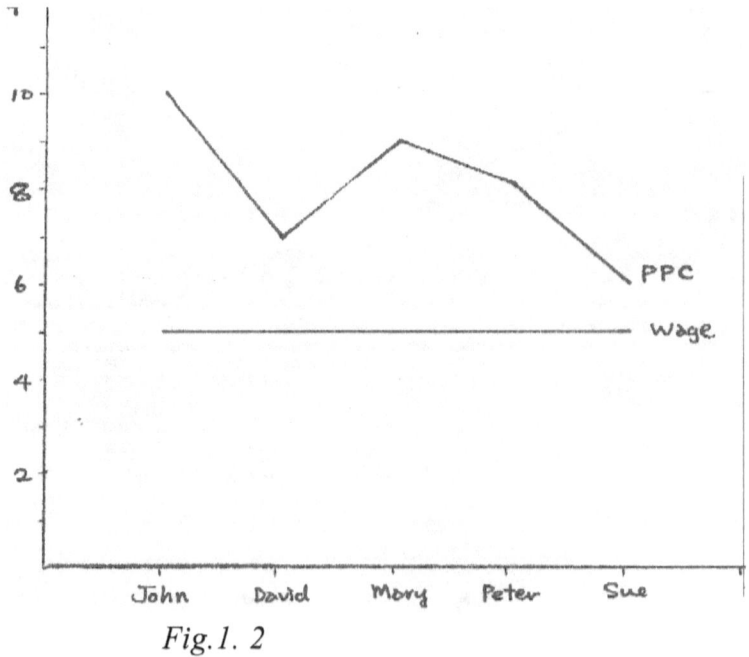

Fig.1. 2

The wage line is always below the potential performance curve (PPC) since companies will lose money if they hire a person whose wage is higher than the return that the person can provide. Just look at the fast-food restaurant as an example. If the employees' wages rise to $7.00 an hour, the situation is shown in figure 1.3.

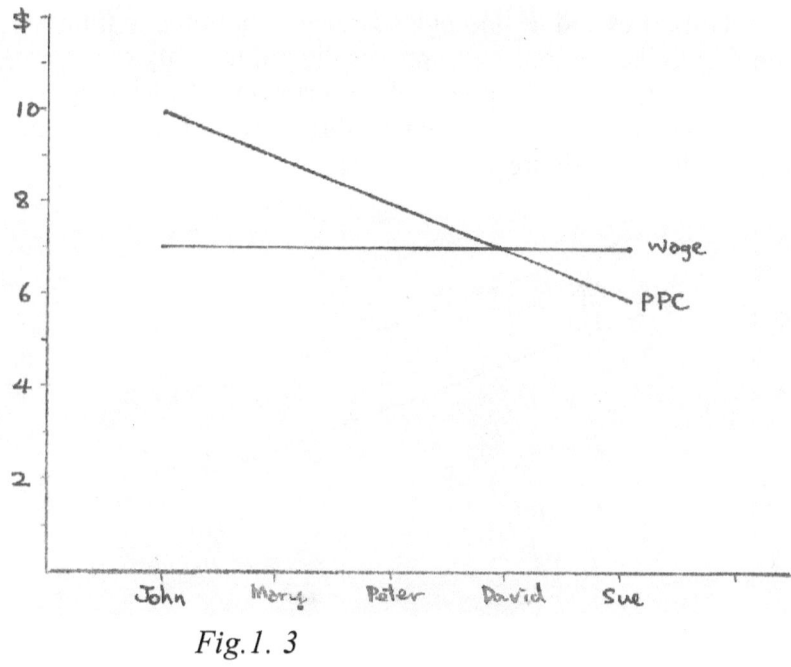

Fig.1. 3

    The wage for Sue is $7.00 an hour, but the maximum return she can provide for her restaurant is only $6.00 an hour. Since the restaurant is losing money by hiring her, the restaurant has no reason to keep her. The restaurant may fire Sue and hire another person who has a higher potential performance.

Change in Potential Performance

    Can the potential performance curve change? Yes. Even though the potential performance is the maximum return of employees, the potential performance can still be changed by other factors, such as technology improvement.

Increase in Potential Performance

1. Technology:

Time flies and technology advances from time to time. Technology, like computers, improves the productivity of many industries. It increases the potential performance of each employee. The potential performance curve will shift upward from PPC1 to PPC2 as follows in figure 1.4.

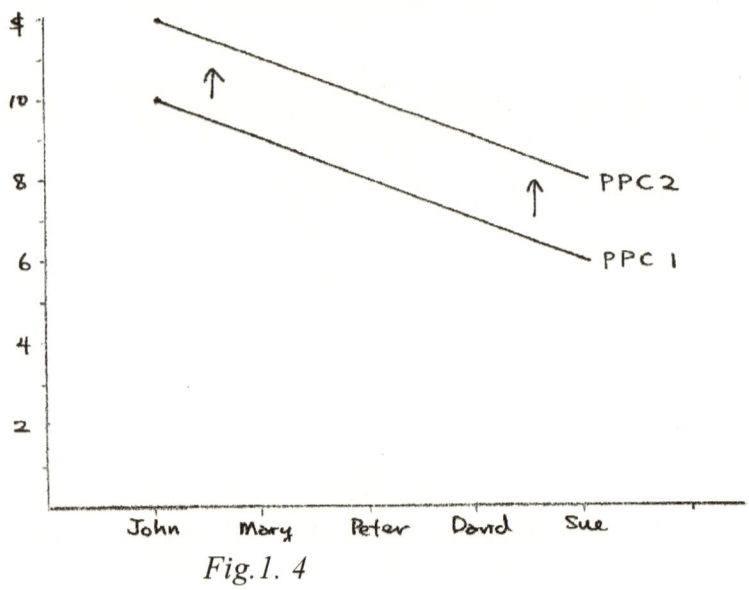

Fig.1. 4

2. Work Experience:

The longer history you have working on the same job, the better quality and return you can provide as a result. That is not difficult to understand. As a new employee has just started his position, he needs time to understand what his job is. Even if he is a certified public accountant who should know the unified format for doing an accounting job, he will still need to learn how to file documents and search old files in the company since different companies have their own styles.

In the fast-food restaurant, John may not flip eggs very smoothly or quickly at the beginning. After he has practiced long enough, he will flip eggs perfectly every time without breaking even one egg. That is what we call work experience. Long-term work experience will result in a high PPC. See figure 1.4. John's PPC will shift upward from PPC1 to PPC2.

Decrease in Potential Performance

It sounds impossible, but when technology goes backward, the overall potential performance of all employees' decreases. The PPC will shift the whole curve downward from PPC1 to PPC2 as seen in figure 1.5 below.

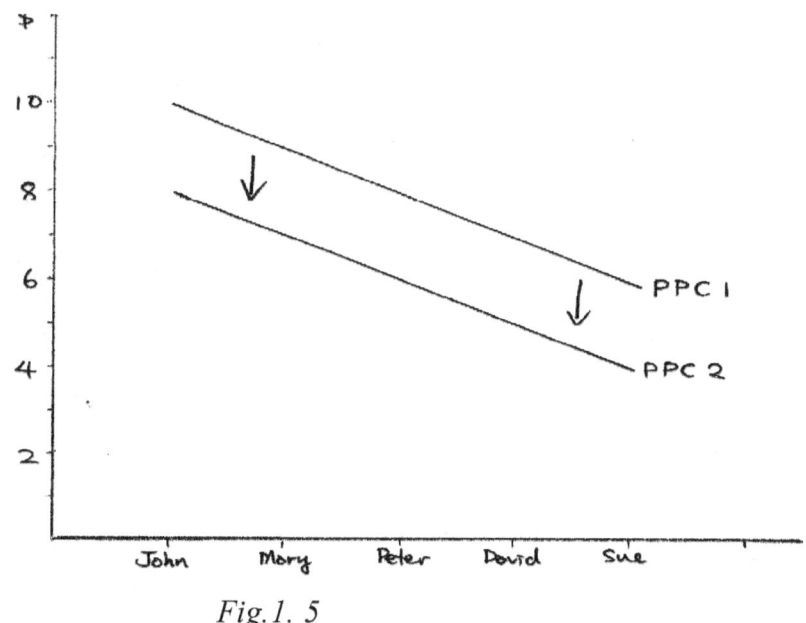

Fig.1. 5

Indeed this did occur, as I remember, before the year 2000. Some people may remember the Y2K bug. It was a software error in which the date in our computer systems would have been in error after the last day of 1999. Therefore, many companies made hard copies to backup documents. Even banks spent a lot of resources on making hard copies of all their accounts, and they spent a lot of man power on solving the software error.

Other than technology moving backward, a natural disaster is also one of the factors that decrease the PPC. Earthquakes, for example, may damage buildings, facilities, and machines. Employees may need to work without any help from these tools.

Or, for some reason, some extra procedure may decrease the PPC, too. Just like in airports where there have been a lot of X-ray machines set up at all the international terminals to check each traveler for any dangerous items in their luggage. This procedure may decrease the PPCs of all employees working in airports. Even the PPC of all the employees from any company who need to travel may also decrease because they will need more time to do business aboard.

Chapter 2

More Concepts for PPC

1.	Potential performance curve is not used to find how many employees should be hired, it is used to find who should be hired or fired. We could use the marginal productivity curve to determine the number of employees to hire. If you wish to know more about marginal productivity (MP), you can find out more about it in economics books. Marginal productivity is very important; economists use it as a demand curve in a factor market.

In PPC, the amount of employed people is not very important to determine; the quality of the employees' work is the main point. For example, the restaurant hired five people before. What if there are another two new people, Chris and Tom? Their PPCs are shown as follows:

Chris	$9/hour
Tom	$7/hour

The graph will be shown as figure 2.1a.

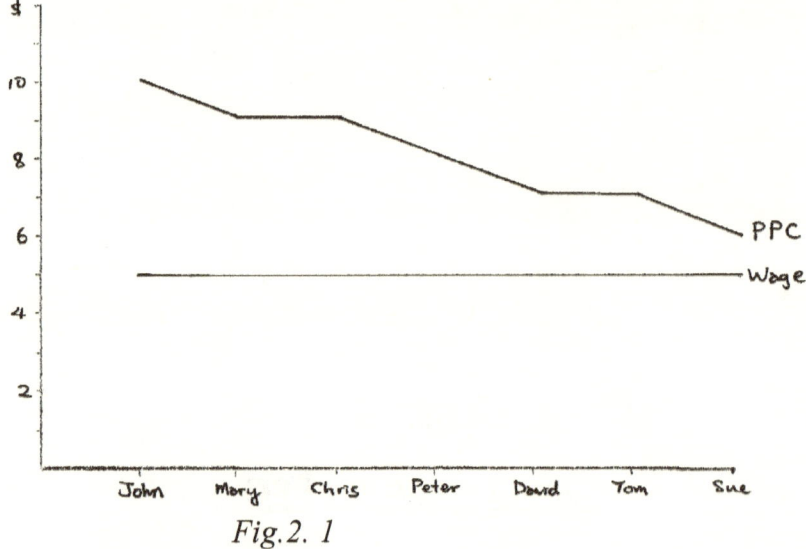

Fig.2. 1

In this case, the company should hire seven people instead of five people.

Marginal productivity theory can determine how many people a company should hire because there is an assumption behind it that all employees are the same. Since the quality of each employee is different, we cannot determine how many people should be hired exactly even if we are using marginal productivity theory. In other words, when the quality of employees is a variable factor, we can only determine who should be hired, but not the exact number of employees who should be hired.

2. In the fast-food restaurant example, we assumed there was no other fixed cost such as rent. Now if we assume the monthly rent is $1000.00, then the hourly rent will be $5.77 ($1000 x 12 / 52 / 40). Therefore, the profit of the restaurant should now be $9.23 ($15 - $5.77).

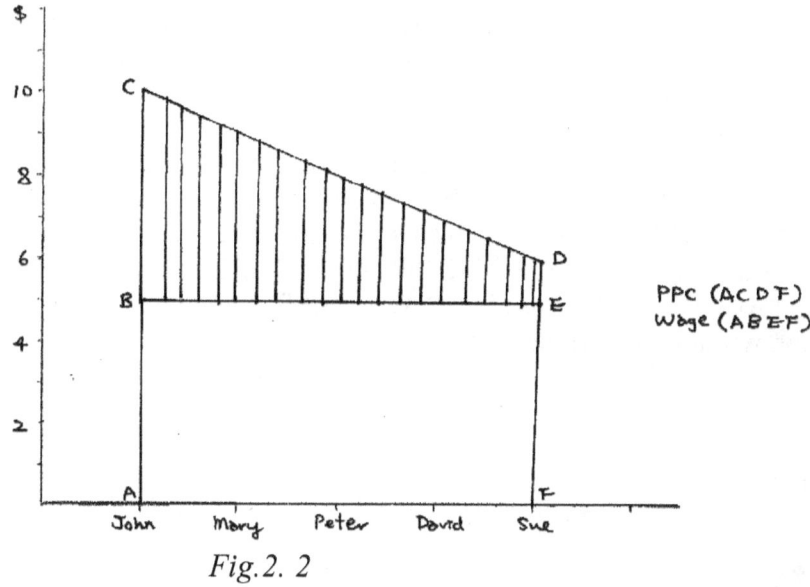

Fig.2. 2

In figure 2.2, the area "BCDE" is the profit for the restaurant before subtracting the rent cost. The total value of this area "BCDE" is $15.00. And the rent cost can be deducted from this area "BCDE". There are some complicated considerations that we will discuss later. The PPC will look like figure 2.3.

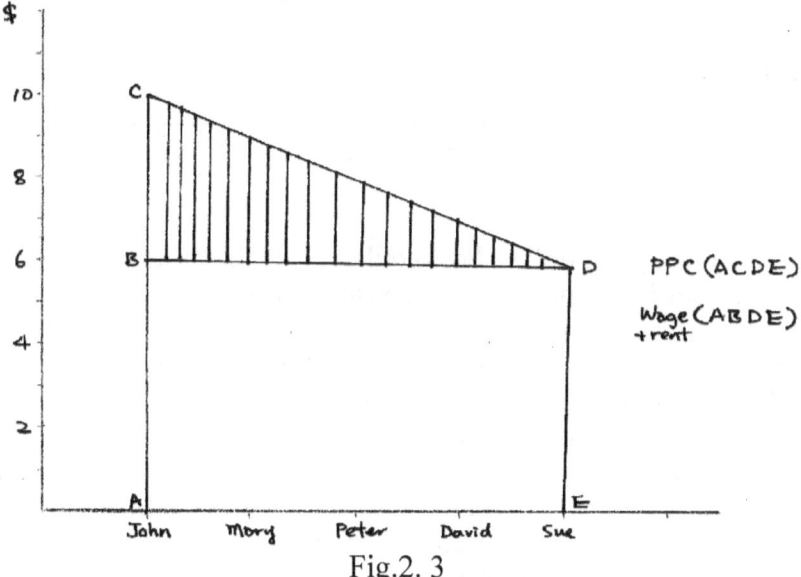

Fig.2. 3

The area "ABDE" will raise $1 ($5.77 / 5 and round it to a dollar) over five employees. In this situation, the boss still does not need to consider if he needs to fire someone.

3. In point 2, I mentioned there are some complicated considerations. Here is one: What if the rent is not $1000.00 per month, but $2000.00 per month? As you can calculate, the hourly rate of the rent will be $11.54 ($2000.00 x 12 / 52 / 40). The cost area "ABDE" will increase by $2.31 for all five employees. The graph will look like figure 2.4.

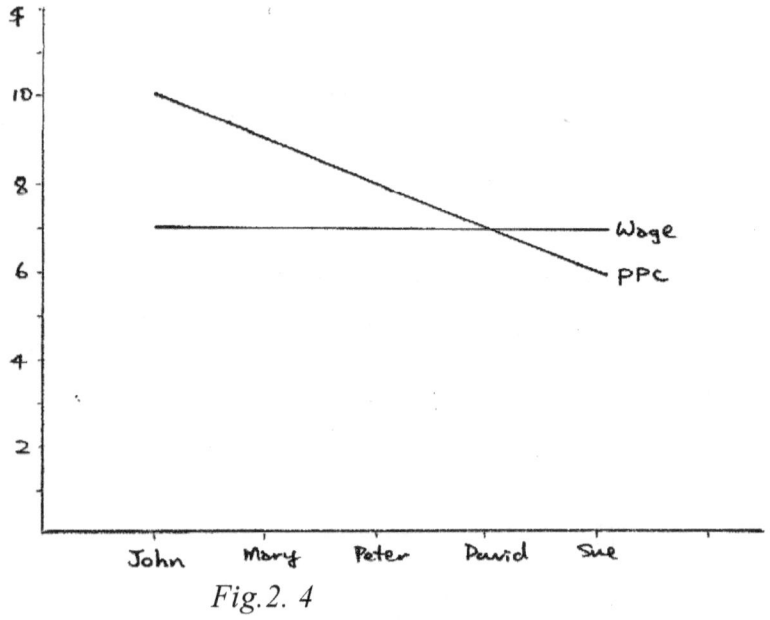

Fig.2. 4

In this situation, the boss could decide that hiring Sue and David causes loss. The boss may consider hiring someone to replace both of them in the long run or hire only three employees: John, Mary, and Peter. However, in the short run it is not that easy to quickly hire someone to replace them or even to just lay someone off. Moreover, let Sue and David go will not solve the problem, neither. If the company just fires two people without a replacement, the fixed cost will be divided by three not five. So the hourly rate rent per employee will be $3.85 ($2000.00 x 12 / 52 / 40 / 3). The graph will look like figure 2.5.

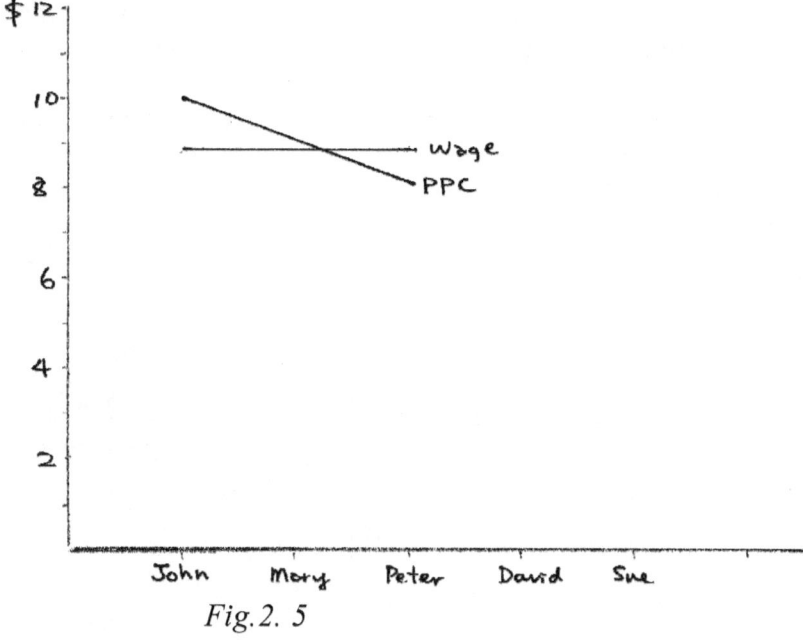

Fig.2. 5

After firing two employees, the average fixed cost will rise. It makes sense for the company to fire Peter now. Then the hourly rate rent per employee will be $5.77 ($2000.00 x 12 / 52 / 40 / 2). The graph will look like figure 2.6.

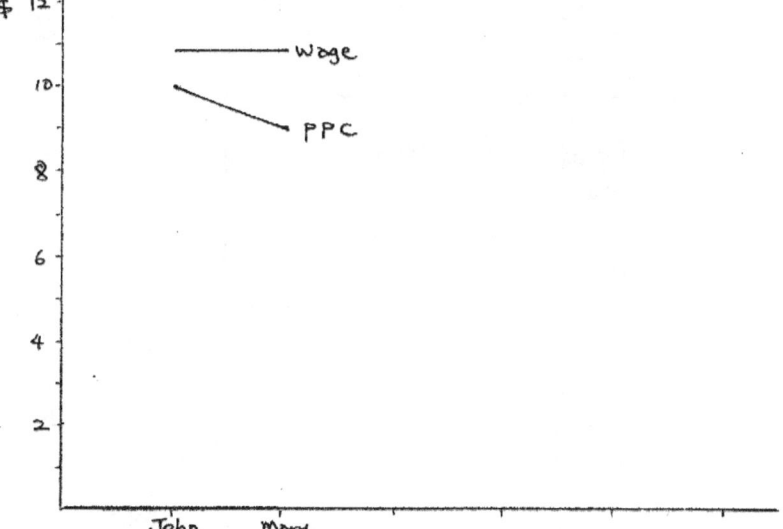

Fig.2. 6

After firing two employees, the average fixed cost will rise again. This time the company will have to fire everyone.

Therefore, firing people may not solve the problem. If that is the case, the company can keep the employees and still make a profit. Then all the cost should only be deducted in the profit area. The graph should look like figure 2.7.

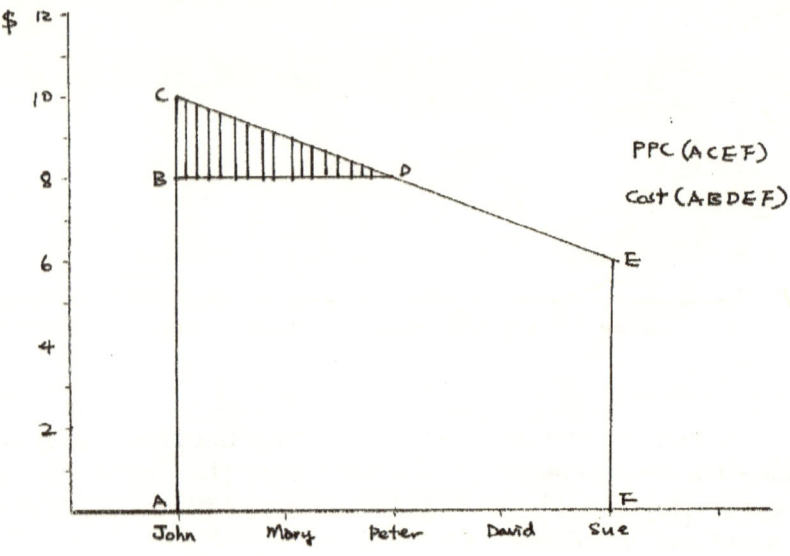

Fig. 2. 7

	PPC	Cost
John	$10.00	$7.85
Mary	$9.00	$7.85
Peter	$8.00	$7.85
David	$7.00	$7.00
Sue	$6.00	$6.00
Total	$40.00	$36.55

The cost, $36.55, will subtract the cost of $6.00 and $7.00 for Sue and David then divide by three for Peter, Mary, and John. The company can still have a tiny hourly profit of $3.45 ($40.00 - $36.55) in this situation. In the long run, the boss can keep the situation like it is or hire someone to replace Sue and David.

Here we can also find the break-even point. Break-even point means an exact point where you can find no profit and no loss. When the fixed cost or other costs are captured in the profit area that means all income is equal to all costs. That is the break-even point. It also implies that if there are any more cost increases, the company should get out of business. See figure 2.8.

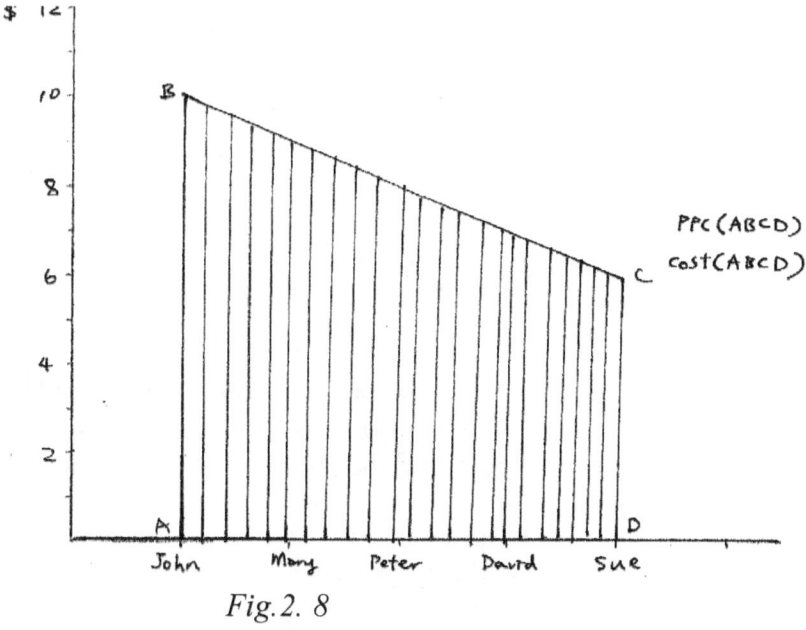

Fig. 2. 8

Fixed cost is a cost that will not change in amount no matter how many employees you hire. However, the average fixed cost will decrease when more employees are hired. See figure 2.9.

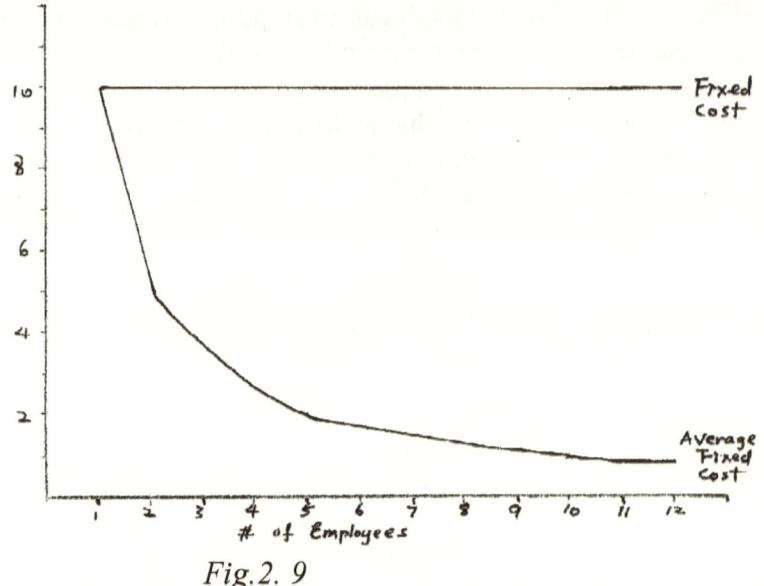

Fig.2. 9

The more employees you hire, the lower the average fixed cost will be. Therefore, the company will hire more employees to minimize the average fixed cost until they reach the maximum of profit.

4.   Point 3 shows the fixed cost. What about variable cost? Variable cost is cost that you need to acquire more of when you want to produce more. A burger restaurant, for example, needs to acquire more beef patties to produce more burgers. A burger needs, at least, one beef patty. Ten burgers need at least ten beef patties. If a burger contains buns and beef only, and the total cost of buns and beef is $1.00 and the price is $2.00 each, then John can produce and sell ten burgers hourly at most, and Mary can produce and sell nine burgers hourly at most. In other words, variable cost is counted inside the PPC already; therefore, the higher the variable cost is, the lower the PPC will be.

5.   A person's PPC in this job is different than the person's PPC in other jobs. Therefore, if a person is not good at this job, or may I say, if a person's PPC in this job is very low, he may have a higher PPC in another job as show in figure 2.10.

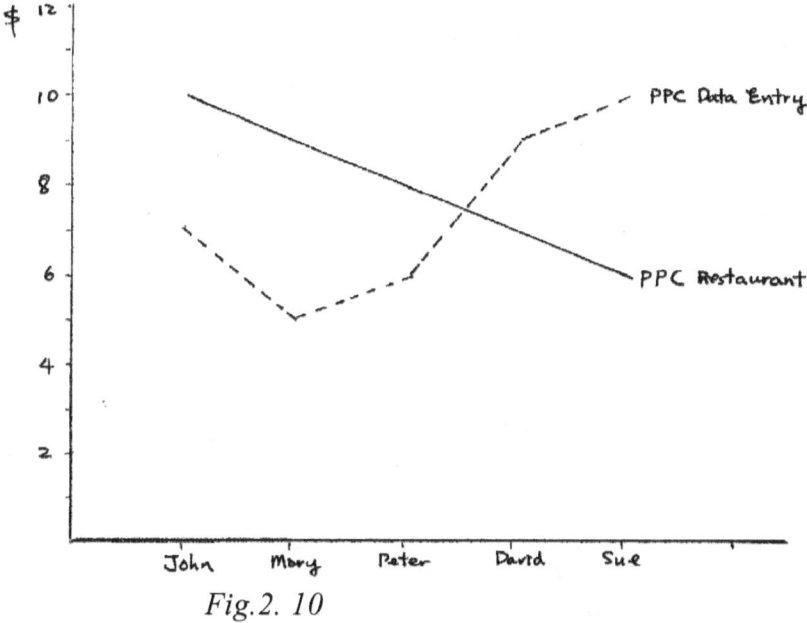
Fig.2. 10

In this case, Sue may be better working in a data entry job, and John may be better off staying at the restaurant.

6. Does the "law of diminishing marginal productivity" exist in PPC?

Yes, it exists. Basically speaking, diminishing marginal return is a fact. It is based on observation. Economists found that under a constant fixed factor situation, increasing a particular variable factor causes increases in products produced. At a certain level, the increasing particular variable factor will eventually cause a decrease in the product produced. It is a fact; we don't need to argue with it.

The law of diminishing marginal productivity returns was first observed in agricultural activities where successive units of farming effort were applied to a given piece of land. David Ricardo used the idea of imperfect factor substitution to create this law.

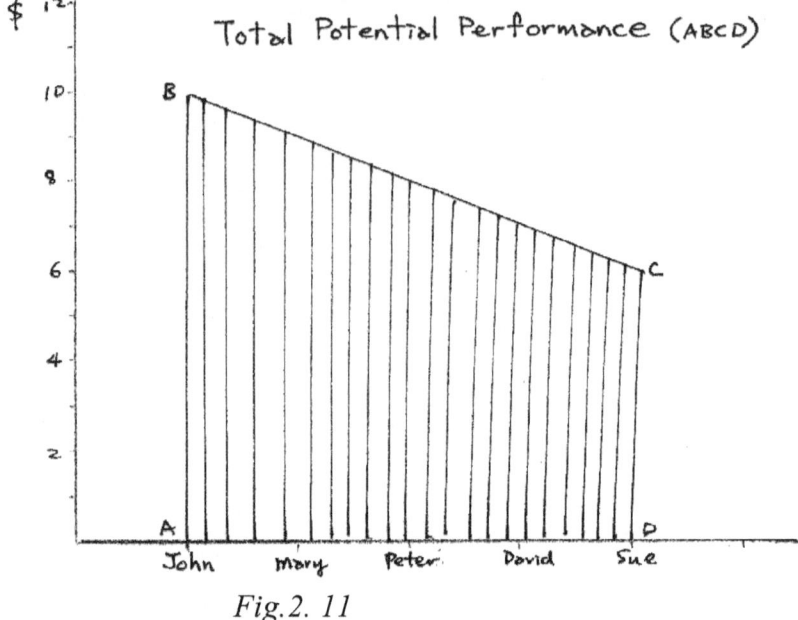

Fig. 2. 11

PPC does reflect this point. When a company hires more and more people (variable factor) in a given place, like a fast-food restaurant (fixed factor), hiring more qualified employees (all employees whose PPC is higher than the wage line) will increase the total shadowed area of PPC, which is the total potential performance (See figure 2.11), until a certain level of increasingly qualified employees is reached. Then the PPC of each employee will decrease, but the level of each employee may vary since each people have a different tolerance in different environments. And the overall PPC will shift downward. Please see figure 2.12.

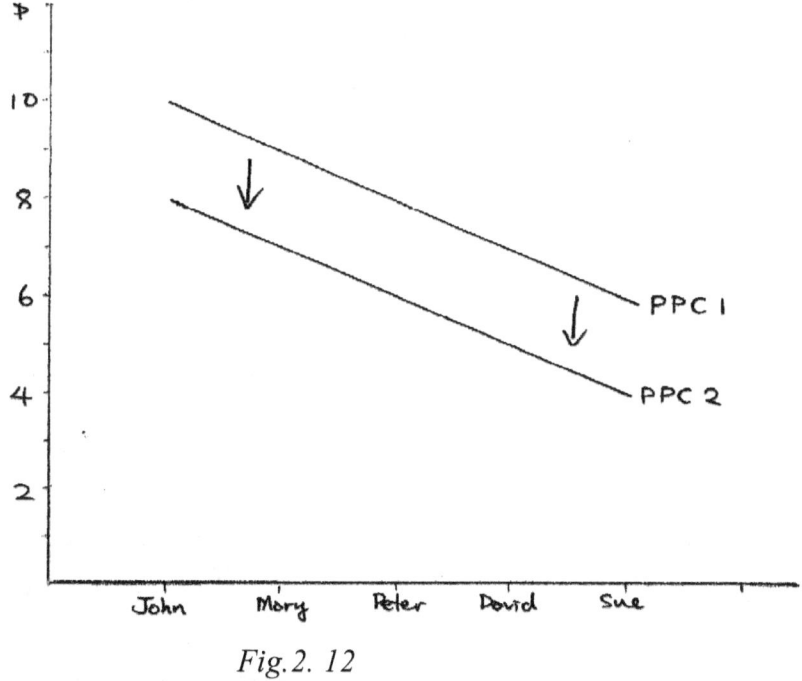

Fig. 2. 12

7. Employment budget for the company.
If the fast-food restaurant has a budget constraint that allows them to only spend $15 per hour on hiring employees, how does the company determine who they are going to hire?

The company has five people that it can choose: John, David, Mary, Peter, and Sue. Please see figure 2.13 and figure 2.14.

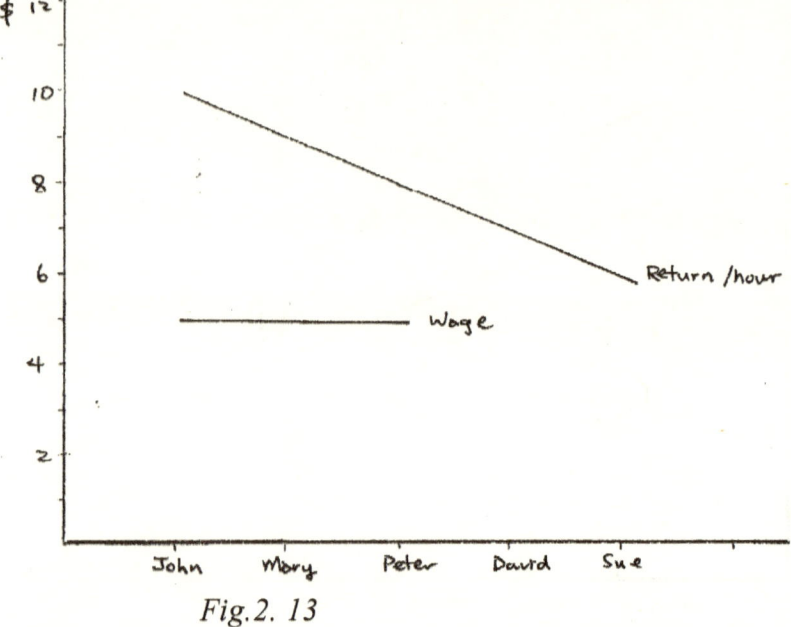

Fig.2. 13

Since the hourly wage for John, Mary, and Peter is $5.00, the total is $15.00 per hour already. Therefore, the restaurant cannot hire David and Sue at the moment. See figure 2.13.

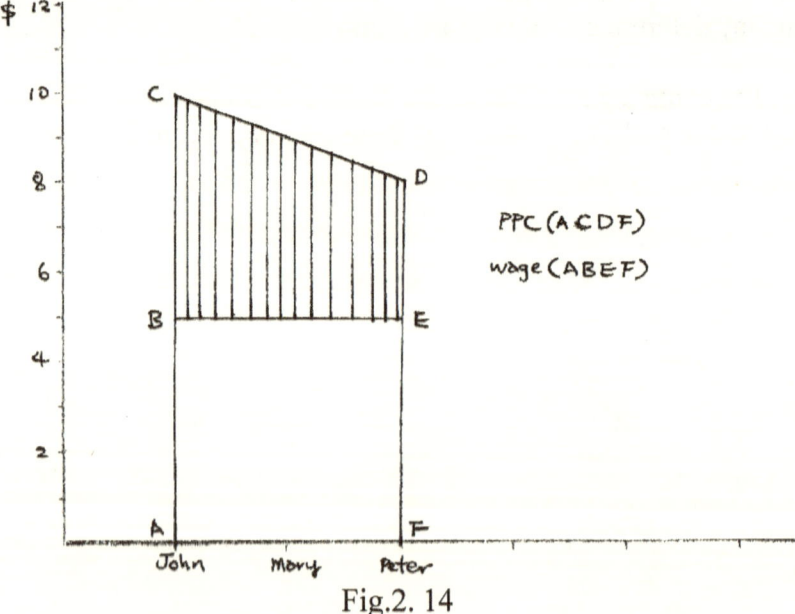

Fig.2. 14

Since the restaurant hired these three people, the restaurant will earn $12.00 per hour ($5.00 + $4.00 + $3.00). See figure 2.14.

As you can see, because we ranked the PPC of these five people at the beginning, it is easier to find out who the restaurant can earn the maximum profit from, or, I should say, the most term economic rent under the given budget constraint. This situation cannot be solved by marginal productivity return theory.

Chapter 3

Considering Selfishness

As I mentioned in chapter 1, the PPC is the maximum return employees can provide. When employees just work at their best without any selfishness, they can provide the return at PPC level. Selfishness, however, is a person's basic instinct. When John knows he is providing $10.00 an hour return for the restaurant and only getting $5.00 an hour wage back, and looking at Sue who provides only $6.00 an hour without any problem, he might consider working just like Sue, or looking for another job that has better pay.

Even if John just likes working hard and still provides $10.00 an hour on return, people like David and Sue might try in some way to stop John from working hard. They might group together and isolate John at work. When John needs any help at work, they might just give John a hard time. A union is a kind of an example (I am sorry I use this as my example.). If I remember it right, there were strikes held by a union of supermarket employees several times in Southern California between 2003 and 2005. The staff blocked the entrance of their supermarket to prevent any other supermarket workers from going to work.

Either way, the actual performance curve (APC) will decrease from APC1 to APC2 and eventually meet the wage line. That means, eventually, the boss or employer will not earn anything in production if the boss or employer does not do anything to prevent this from happening. Here the APC is a curve showing the actual return that employees provide. This APC must be lower than the PPC since employees cannot provide more return than their maximum potential. It is logical consistency. The curve is shown as figure 3.1.

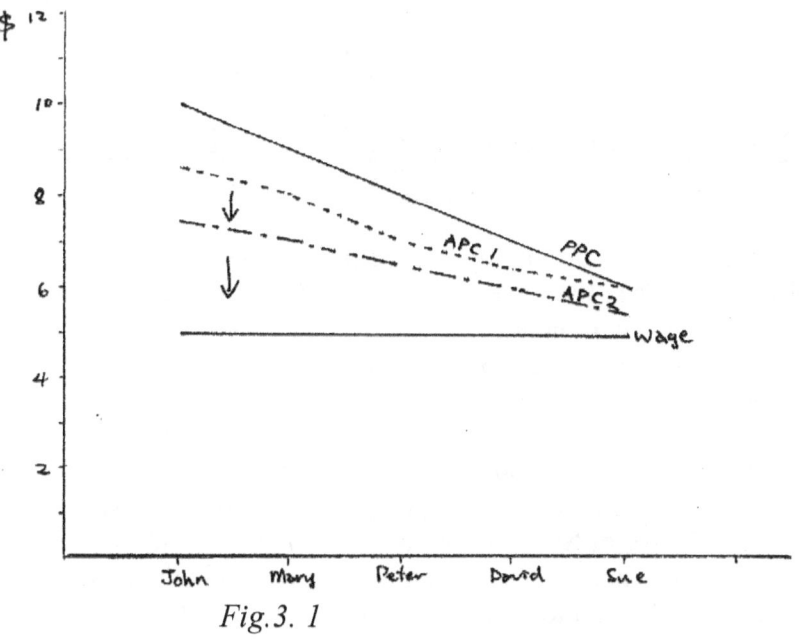

Fig.3. 1

Figure 3.1 shows the APC has decreased from APC1 to APC2, and it will decrease until it reaches the wage line.

Chapter 4

How Do Employers Deal with PPC & Push Up the APC?

Being a boss or employer and finding out all of his employees' PPCs at the lowest cost is the most important job, since it determines his own income. Normally, as I observed, employers may do, but are not limited to, some of the things shown below to figure out the PPC.

1. Wages are a secret among employees. This may have been written in some companies' employee handbooks. So when John looks at David or Sue working lazily, John may think it is because the wages of David and Sue are not so high, leading David and Sue not to work with wholeheartedly. John may never know that their wages are the same as his. He will never feel their pay is unfair because he will never know what it is.

2. Keep giving a lot of jobs to the newly hired employee without considering the employee's ability until the newly hired employee cannot do anymore within the probation period. This was true even in ancient times. The officer or landlord would force slaves to work. If a slave worked a little bit slower or just took a rest, the officer or landlord would hit them until the slave got up to work again or couldn't get up anymore. See paradox of exploitation for more details. In figure 4.1, the PPC for

employees will shift upward and become closer and closer to PPC.

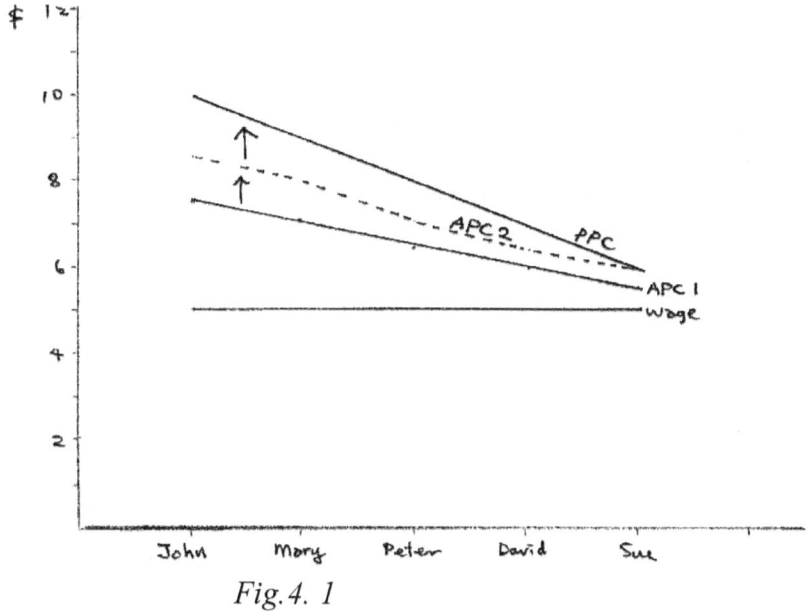

Fig. 4. 1

When all of these new employees pass their probation period, they cannot just stop working hard since the boss knows their abilities already. That means the employees' PPCs have been shown to the employer during the period of probation.

3. Bosses or employers always offer the fantasy of a best employee award, promotion, or wage raise to employees if they work harder.

   A. <u>Best Employee Award:</u>
   A best employee award is an award to the best employee. People in the company have to fight or compete with each other to be the best and get the award. The prize may be a piece of paper, a trophy, a metal, a parking space, or even a bonus. You name it. The main point is, only one person can get the award in a given period of time.

If the award program runs well, the competitors will push their APCs closer and closer to their PPC. However, those employees who are at the edge of the lowest PPC know they will not have a chance to be the winner, and they will not really participate in the award program. These employees may not push their APC to meet their PPC, or, in some cases, they may even pull their APCs down closer and closer to the wage line. The company's APC in this case may look like figure 4.2.

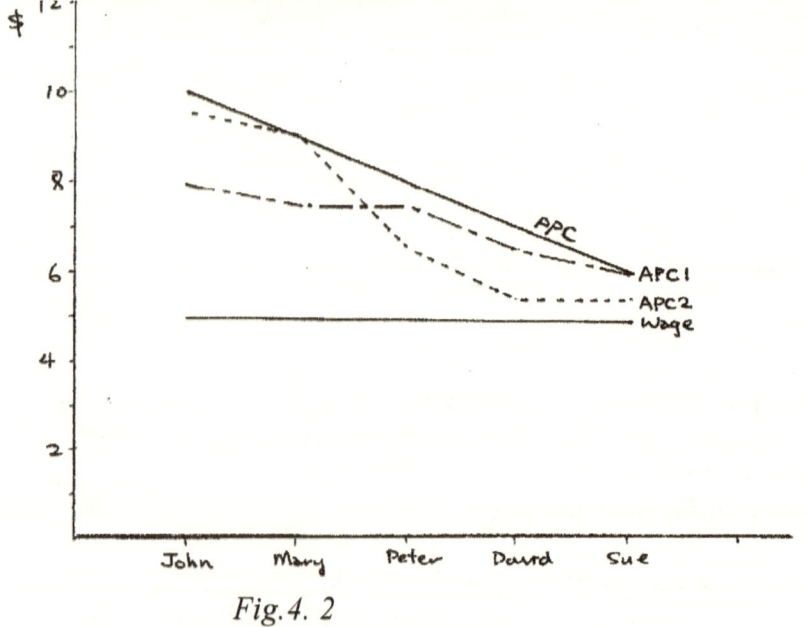

Fig. 4.2

During the time that the award program runs, the APC will change from APC1 to APC2 in figure 4.2. It is very clear that John and Mary are the only two real competitors in the award program. Peter, David, and Sue have given up the competition already.

The situation we mentioned above is a good scenario. This kind of award program only rewards the best employee. It does not mean the employee has the highest PPC. He or she can just do something to make other competitors lower their APCs as I mentioned in the introduction. That something could be legal or illegal, like planting a virus into a competitor's computer system, sending a spy to get a competitor's updated competition process, boycotting, blackmail, and so on. In that case, the overall APC will be closer to the wage line. See figure 4.3 below.

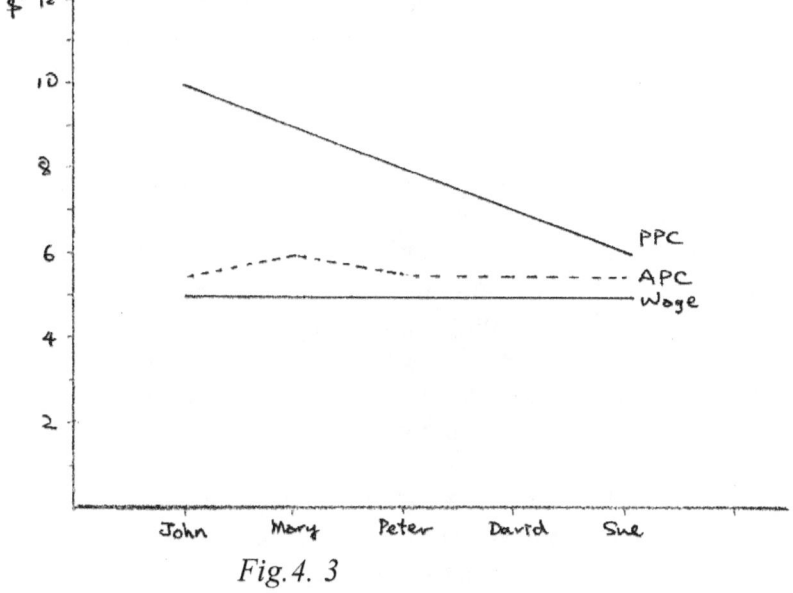

Fig. 4. 3

In the case of figure 4.3, Mary may use blackmail or use some other method to make the other competitors stop working hard in the award program. Therefore, Mary does not need to be very good at her job, or to even work hard for the award. All she needs to do is just have a little better performance than the others. That is enough. Since the situation is controlled by Mary, the competition is not really a competition anymore.

In the big picture, this kind of award program may not help a company to find or reach the PPC. It may even hinder the company in finding it. To run this kind of award program more effectively, I suggest planting hardworking culture into employees' brains first to build a hardworking atmosphere in the workplace. Then the company should try to have better control over the competition to set a fair environment. This may generate a better effect from the award program.

B. Promotion:
Promotion is, of course, a kind of award for the good employee. When there is a higher position available, a bunch of employees will show their good job to their supervisor or boss. They compete with each other for the higher position. A higher position means more power and higher wages. It is similar to the best employee award.

Just like the best employee award, in a good scenario, only a few top employees may take part in the competition. Those employees who never have a chance to be the winner will keep acting normally or even become less enthusiastic on the job. These employees will get lower APCs from time to time. In a bad scenario, even the top performance employee may use some method to make other competitors stop having good performances.

Of course, there are some difference between promotion and the best employee award. The best employee award can run whenever the company wants, no matter how many times a year. However, a promotion, normally, can only occur when there is a position available.

I said "normally" because nowadays a company may create a lot of unnecessary positions just to have enough higher positions to give away, so they can encourage employees to work hard for their promotions all the time. That creates another problem: the ratio between staff and management will be unbalanced. But this is another topic related to business administration. I will not discuss that topic anymore.

C. A Raise:
The "raise" we are talking about is a wage raise, not a raise for all employees, but only those employees who have good performance (i.e., those employees have higher APC will have a raise or bonus.)

A raise is a wage increase continuously over time. See figure 4.4.

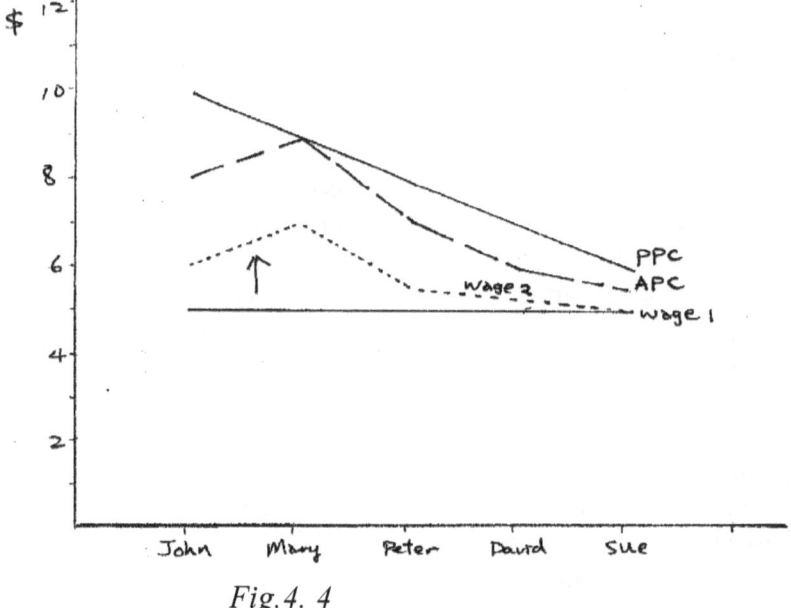

Fig.4. 4

Before, all five employees had wages of $5.00 per hour. A year later, the boss has a better idea of each of the employees' performance (APC). He decides to give raises according to each employee's performance. Since what the boss can see is what the employees have done over the last year, he can only see the employees' APC. Over the last year, Mary worked the hardest and created the most return on the same job, therefore, she gets the highest raise on wage from $5.00 to $7.00 per hour. John has the highest PPC, but he did not fully perform to his best ability, so he only got a raise of $1.00 per hour to become a $6.00 wage per hour earner. Sue, it seems, created the least return on the job. The boss decided not to give her a raise on her wage.

A bonus is an amount or a percentage of the income given away as a prize for one-time only. Since it is not hourly, it will not be shown on the graph.

Of course, to give a raise on a wage or a bonus, employees' wages should continue to be a secret. Although no secret about wages can encourage poorly performing employees to work harder for better raises in the future, no one can tell the efficiency. What if poorly performing employees feel hopeless and perform even worse? What if the employees who perform well are not satisfying the rate of their raise compared to other employees? I would prefer keeping wages a secret between employees still, so that an employee with a higher wage increase will think he is special, and an employee with a lower raise will only know he has a raise. To the one employee who does not have a raise at all, he will think that is normal.

4. By telling employees how tight the company's budget is and that layoffs may happen someday not far away, employees will always be afraid to be on the edge of APC. When layoffs do happen, those employees on the edge will be the first group of people to be considered for layoffs. Therefore, all employees on the edge will try their best to be away from the edge.

A company having a tight budget can have a lot of different meanings.

A. Increase in Variable Cost:

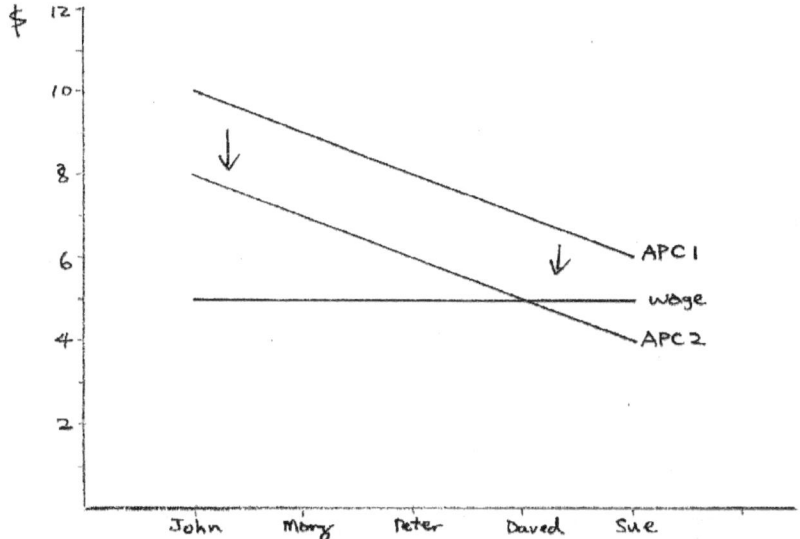

Fig.4. 5

In chapter 2, we mentioned that the variable cost should be counted in employees' APCs. Figure 4.5 shows the APC has decreased from APC1 to APC2 because of the increase in variable cost of production. That will lead to a layoff. Here we are talking about just always giving employees the idea of being laid off. We just added an imaginary extra variable cost, which we set at $2.00 per hour for each employee on the production. Sue worked the hardest to get off the edge of the layoff list, and her APC is $8.00 per hour now. In other words, her imaginary extra variable cost APC is $6.00 per hour. David is the one on the edge of the layoff list now as shown in figure 4.6.

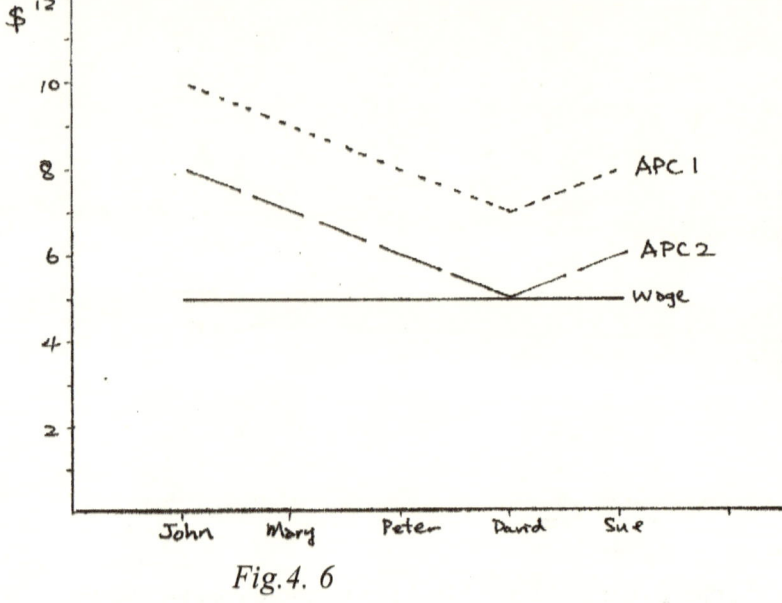

Fig. 4. 6

B. Increase in Fixed Cost:

In chapter 2 we mentioned that the fixed cost should be capturing the company's profit area. It is the blue area in figure 4.7.

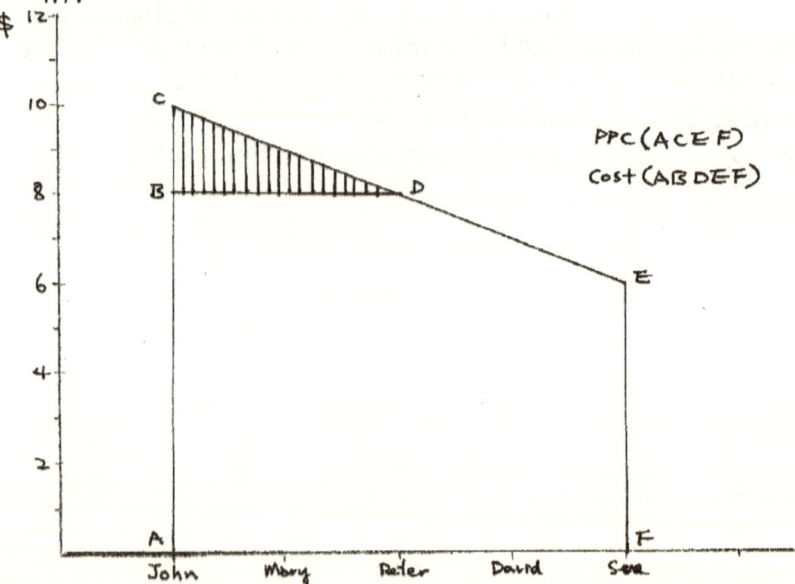

Fig. 4. 7

When the company mentions that the budget is tight in this way, it means the company thinks the shadow area "BCD" is too small. So the company will think of hiring more employees with higher APCs. Here Chris and Tom join the company as shown in figure 4.8.

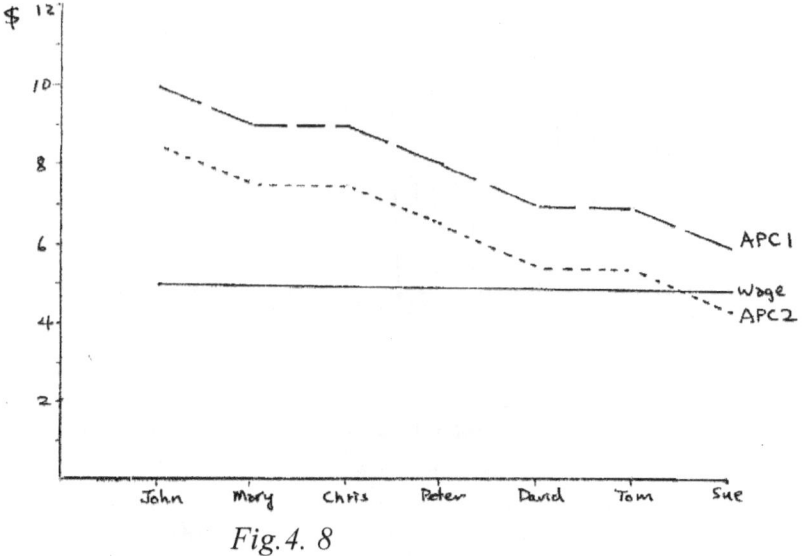

Fig. 4. 8

Since Chris and Tom joined the company, the APC should be APC1 in figure 4.8. However, there is the factor of diminishing marginal productivity return, the overall APCs of all employees decrease from APC1 to APC2. In figure 4.8, you can see that Sue's APC2 is lower than the wage line. That means Sue is on the layoff list.

C. Cost is Bigger than the Break-even Point:

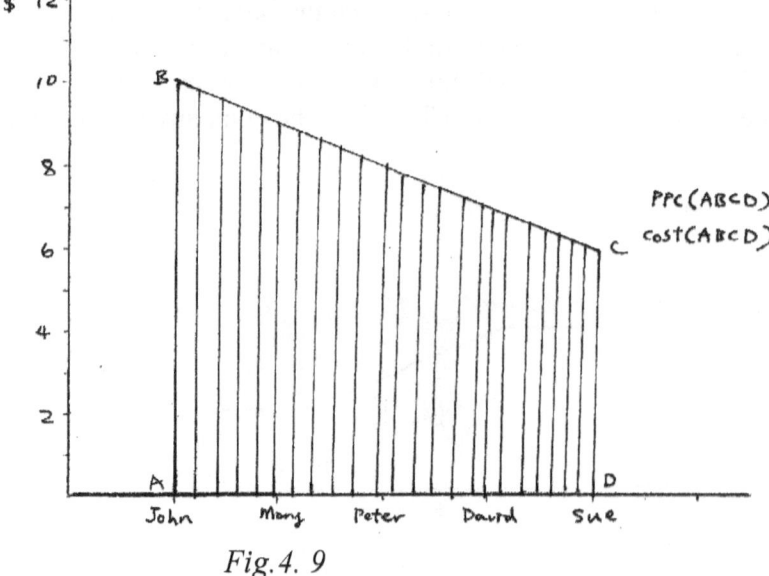

Fig. 4. 9

Figure 4.9 shows the break-even point. That happens when the total income is equal to the total cost. If the total cost is less than the total income by $1.00 that means the company still earns $1.00. If the total cost is bigger than the total income by $1.00 that means the company has lost $1.00 and the company should be out of the business. Since the company is out of business, layoffs, of course, occurred.

In either of the above examples, the lower APC employees will improve their APCs to keep their jobs. How about those employees in the top group? Since the lower APC employees are working hard regardless of the actual number of their APCs, the higher APC employees can see that. It will encourage the higher APC employees to continue to work hard. The whole atmosphere in the workplace will improve.

5. "Efficiency wage" is defined as a higher than market-clearing wage set by employers.

   I am using the fast-food restaurant as an example. See figure 4.10.

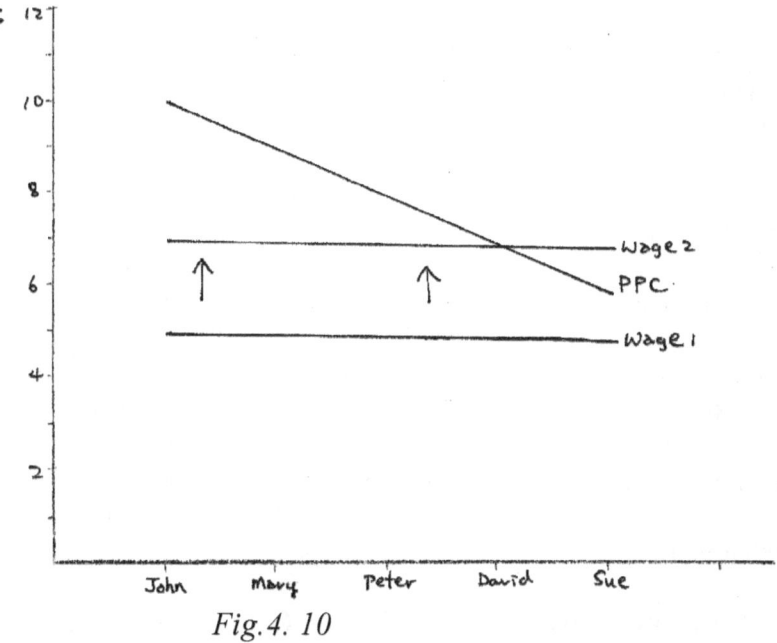

Fig. 4. 10

The market wage is set at the level of wage1, which is $5.00 per hour, and the restaurant set its wage at wage 2, which is $7.00 per hour. The reason the company set this efficiency wage is because the company wants to let employees know that they cannot find this wage level at other companies. The employees will have to work harder to avoid being fired. The higher the efficiency wage, the higher the cost to shirk.

In the PPC theory, this efficiency wage may or may not be as good as they think. You can see after the wage level is set at $7.00, Sue will be fired or laid off since she is not able to provide service at a value equal to or higher than the wage. In this way, the standard return of production in the restaurant has been set at $7.00 per hour. In other words, each of employees will shirk less. Like John shirked $5.00 per hour before ($10-$5), now he shirks $3.00 per hour ($10-$7). So what?

John has the highest PPC in the restaurant. He can still see David is providing $7.00 per hour at a maximum since that is David's PPC level. It seems David is still working in the restaurant without any problem. John can provide service worth

$10.00 per hour, but there is no reason he should still provide that much. He could just shirk and produce as little as David. The efficiency wage does improve something: the overall quality of service increases to $7.00 from $5.00 per hour. But that doesn't mean all employees will work without shirking their responsibilities. John will shirk and decrease his APC down to the $7.00 per hour level.

In addition, the efficiency wage may even create more social problems when people like Sue are willing to accept a lower wage but still cannot find a job because most companies tend to hire people having higher PPCs with higher wage wishes. It just doesn't make sense. In the long run, if most companies tend to set the efficiency wage at $7.00 per hour, will the market wage rise from $5.00 to $7.00 eventually? If so, what is the point of the efficiency wage?

Nowadays, most big companies like Google and Microsoft hire people from top universities for very high-level salaries. Most people dream of working for them. So they get good grades and try to get into these firms. They have better knowledge on the job, but that does not necessarily mean they work wholeheartedly without shirking their responsibilities. They may shirk less than $2.00 per hour when their wage rises from $5.00 to $7.00. However, if the PPC of the employee is $10.00 per hour like John's, the company still cannot capture the $3.00 per hour ($10 - $7). Those companies are just getting what they are paying for.

Well, I guess there are only two benefits for the company concerning the efficiency wage. The first one is lower turnover. If an employee does not work for this company, they will have difficulty finding another job to match that wage level in the short run. Employees tend to stay at the job where they are at. But, again, it does not mean they will work wholeheartedly without shirking a bit. Only David in the fast-food restaurant situation will work wholeheartedly since his PPC is equal to the wage line. If David does not work wholeheartedly, his productivity will be less than the wage level, and he will definitely be fired very soon. Lower turnover is not a good way to find out the PPCs of employees and capture it. I will explain that later in this chapter.

The second benefit is the improvement in the basic standard. If employees are waiters or waitresses, their basic service standard will rise from $5.00 to $7.00. That means their overall performance on their jobs, including their working attitude, how they treat customers, and so on will be improved by $2.00 per hour. Nothing more! And this $2.00 extra standard actually is paid by the company itself.

If the company can use some other ways to push people to work closer to their PPCs, the company can save this $2.00 per hour extra and capture it as the company's economic rent or profit. Therefore, I don't recommend companies using the efficiency wage as a way to encourage employees to work harder.

6. Reference from a third party

An employee's history may tell us how the person handled his job before, so the employer can estimate how the employee will handle his job after he has been hired. It is a way to lower the information cost on finding the PPC of an employee. If the employee had a good reputation on his previous job, at least the employer can have higher expectations of the employee. If the employee was fired because of low-functioning in a previous job and his wage was $5.00 per hour like Sue's in the fast-food restaurant example, the employer can guess that the PPC of this employee may be around $5.00. Therefore, a reference is useful, and a lot of companies will require applicants to provide such information on their applications.

The problem is that a reference is a subjective item. You can say you prefer an apple to an orange, but you cannot say that you like an apple more than I do. Another question is: How real is the information in the reference. The third party may provide unreal reference information about the employee for some reason, like the third party may be the employee's ex-boss and father. The third party may be the employee's friend also. We should use this information with caution.

7. Related to point 6, headhunters exist

A headhunter is an agent who hires people for companies. In olden times, companies would go to agencies to post a position. Headhunters would find people or people would go to them to fill the vacancy. Nowadays, headhunters are not just providing a platform between employees and employers; they are also providing information, training, and comparisons for employees and employers. I believe most agencies will link with universities, other education institutions, and private investigators to provide more useful and accurate information in the future.

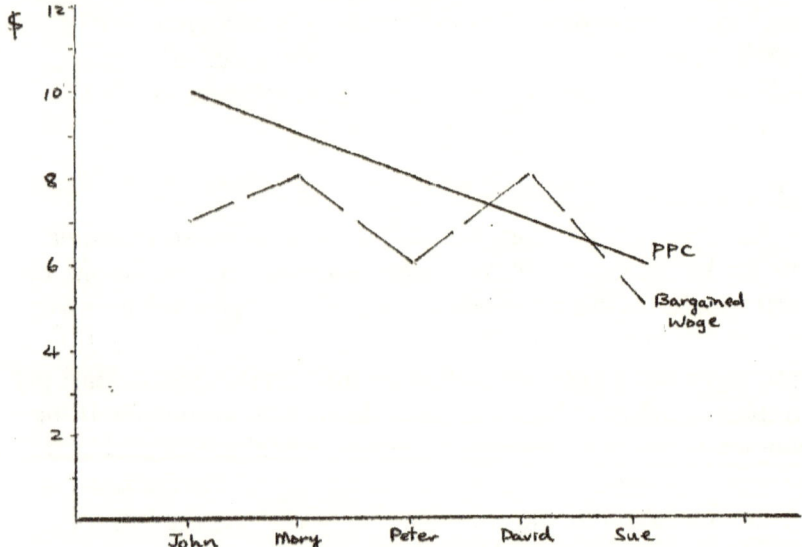

Fig.4. 11

Headhunting is a two-way job. They can represent either employees or employers. They bargain the wage level of each employee. See figure 4.11. Through the bargaining procedure, the wage level may sometimes be even higher than the PPC, since only the employee knows what the PPC is at the beginning of employment. However, the employer will figure it out during the probation period, and the new employee whose wage level is higher than the PPC like David's in figure 4.11 will be fired as soon as possible, or the employer will be forced to lower his wage level.

8. Turnover

Low turnover in a company is a good point for attracting people to join the company. However, on the company's side, companies should prefer having higher turnover to pursue higher economic rent. In PPC theory, as we mentioned before, when there is no diminishing marginal productivity issue yet, we do not really focus on the number of people the company should hire; we actually focus on the level of each employee's PPC.

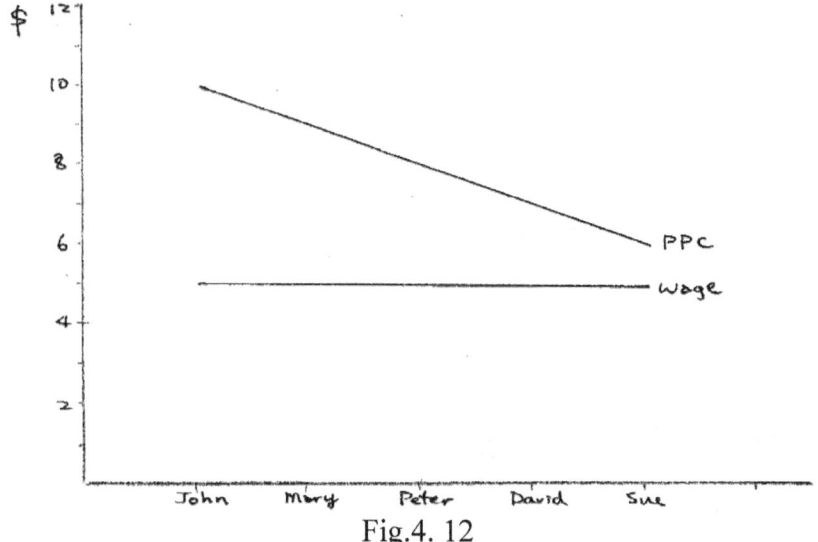

Fig.4. 12

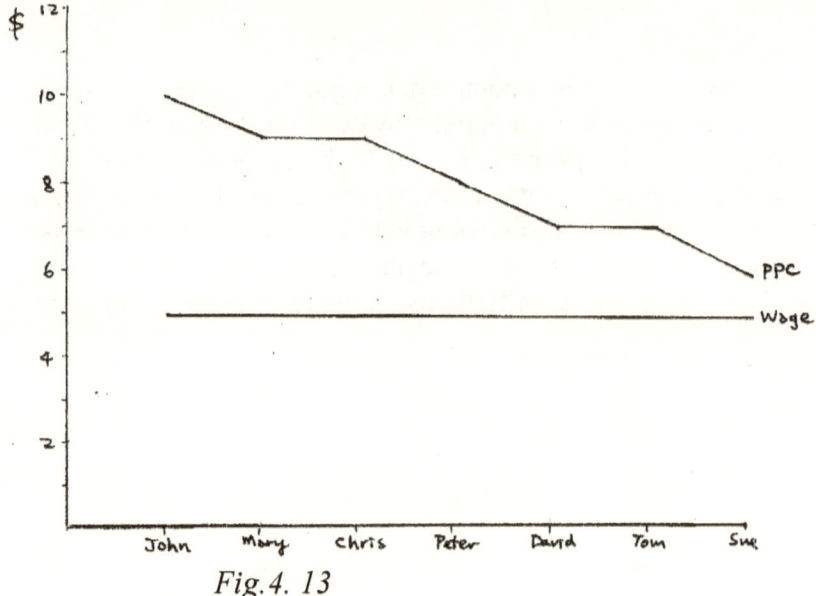

Fig. 4. 13

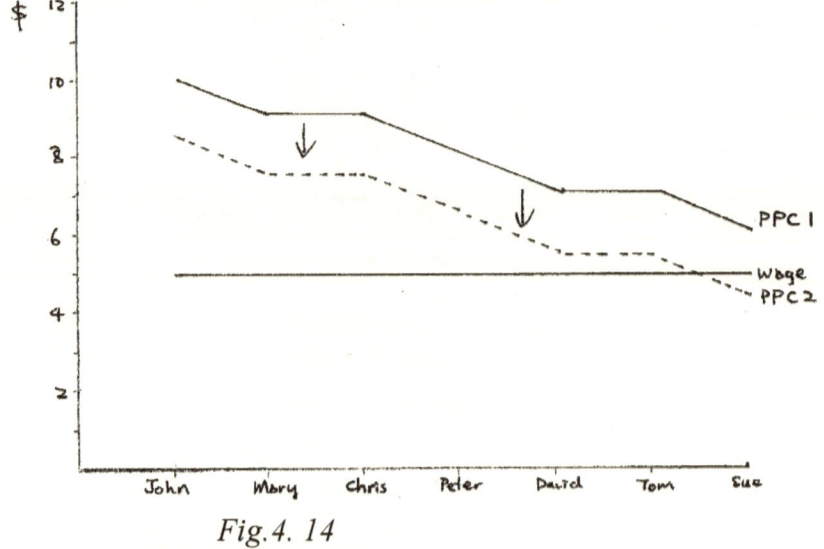

Fig. 4. 14

In figure 4.12, the company hires five people, and the company earns $15.00 per hour economic rent ($5+$4+$3+$2+$1). In figure 4.13, the company hires seven people (add Chris and Tom), and the company earns $21.00 per hour economic rent ($5+$4+$4+$3+$2+$2+$1).

However, after a certain amount of employees have been hired, the diminishing marginal productivity will apply. When it applies, the PPC will shift downward, the level of each employee on diminishing marginal productivity will vary. We make it an equal amount to make explaining the theory easier. See figure 4.14. The company fires Sue, and the diminishing marginal productivity causes the overall productivity to be reduced. The company will only hire six people (Sue was fired) and the company will earn $11.00 per hour economic rent ($3.5+$2.5+$2.5+$1.5+$0.5+$0.5). Since the total economic rent of the company is reduced, they may consider firing Tom also to keep the size of the staff limited to five people. See figure 4.15.

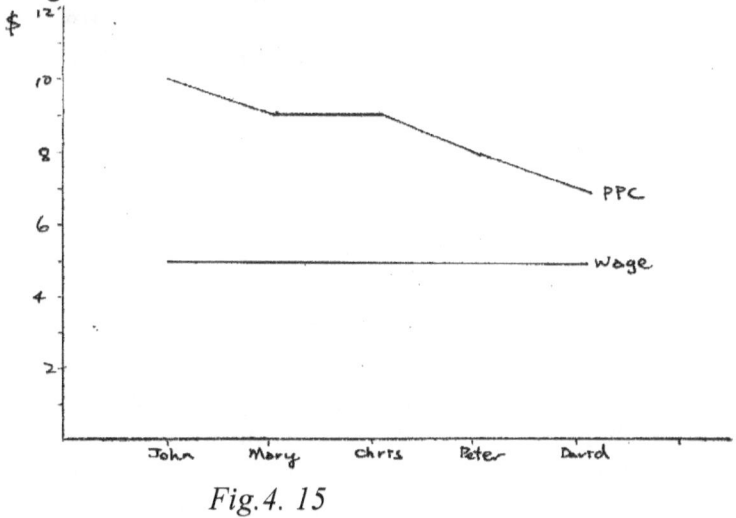

Fig.4. 15

The total economic rent for this combination of employment will be $18.00 per hour ($5+$4+$4+$3+$2). The company hires Chris and Tom, then fires Sue and Tom, and earns an extra $3.00 per hour.

Therefore, keeping a high turnover rate gave the company a chance to choose employees with better PPCs. On the other hand, employees will also feel the pressure to work harder to avoid being on the edge of the PPC.

9. Quota

Some companies, like in the banking industry or insurance industry, have a quota system. Employees are required to reach a certain amount of sales then they can keep their jobs or earn their income. See figure 4.16.

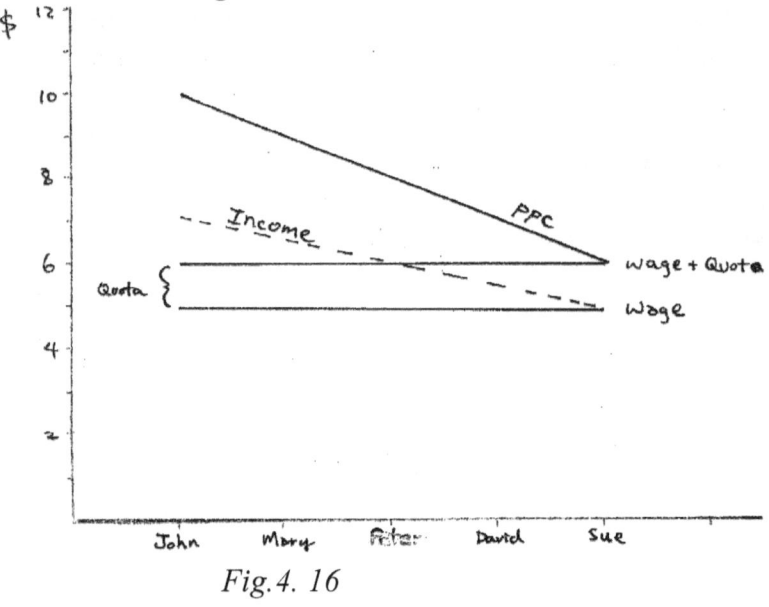

Fig.4. 16

We have been using the fast-food restaurant as an example, and now we are changing it to an insurance company. All five employees have base salaries of $5.00 per hour and receive 50 percent of any sales after reaching a $6.00 target. If all five employees work without shirking their responsibilities, they all work at their PPC levels, and they all reach the target $6.00 per hour. Then John's income will be $7.00 per hour ($5 + ($10 - $6) x 50%), and $6.50 for Mary, $6.00 for Peter, $5.50 for David, and $5.00 for Sue.

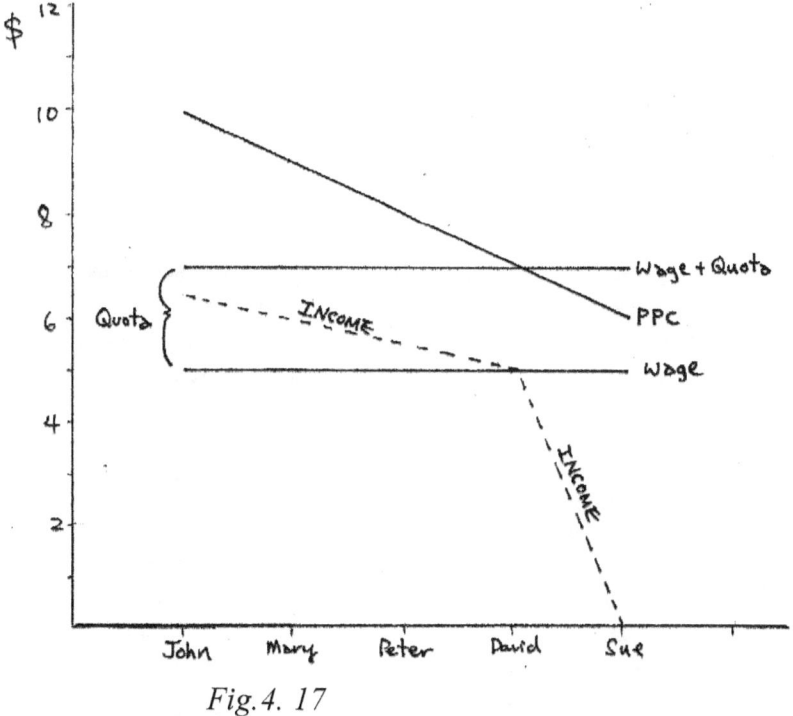

Fig. 4. 17

If the company sets the quota at the level of $7.00 per hour and 50 percent commission for all sales after a $7.00 per hour target (figure 4.17), John will get $6.50, Mary will get $6.00, Peter will get $5.50, David will get $5.00 per hour, and Sue will get nothing, and she may be fired soon.

Of course, employees will not provide their services to a company at their PPC levels. If there is no 50 percent commission and they shirk their responsibilities, they will at least provide their services up to the quota level of $7.00. So they all will get $5.00 per hour, except Sue since her PPC did not reach the quota. See figure 4.18.

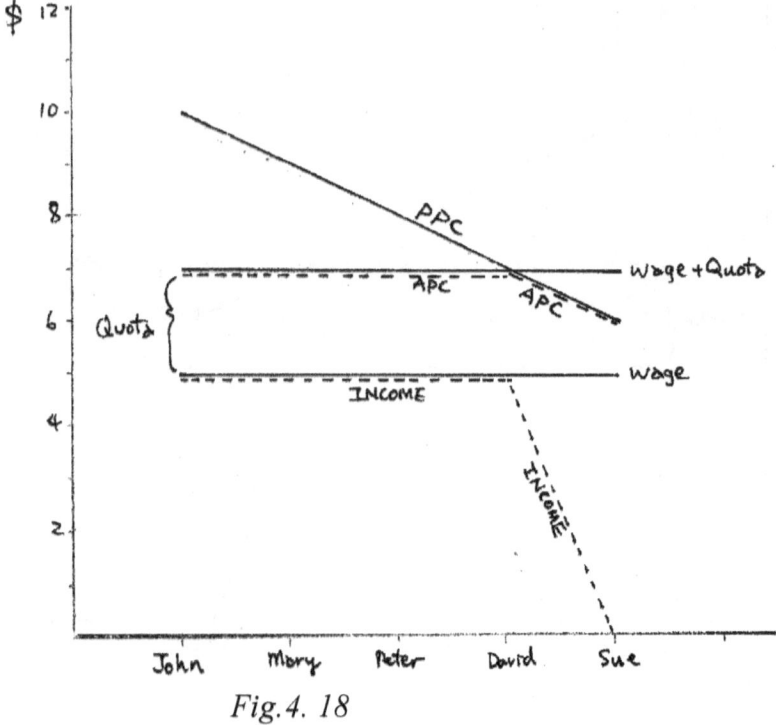

Fig. 4.18

So, what is the point? The point is that the company does not necessarily worry about the employees' PPCs; all employees have been given the target. If they don't reach the target, they don't earn the income. Therefore, the company has control over its economic rent.

By adding the 50 percent commission policy, the company may encourage employees to work at their PPC levels to get more income. This policy will act as an incentive for employee income.

10. Profit sharing

Profit sharing means sharing the profit. The company gives up a percentage of profit to employees. Normally it is like the commission we just mentioned in point 9. Since employees can earn a portion of what they make for the company, they will try working harder for more income. This will push employees work to PPC level. See figure 4.19.

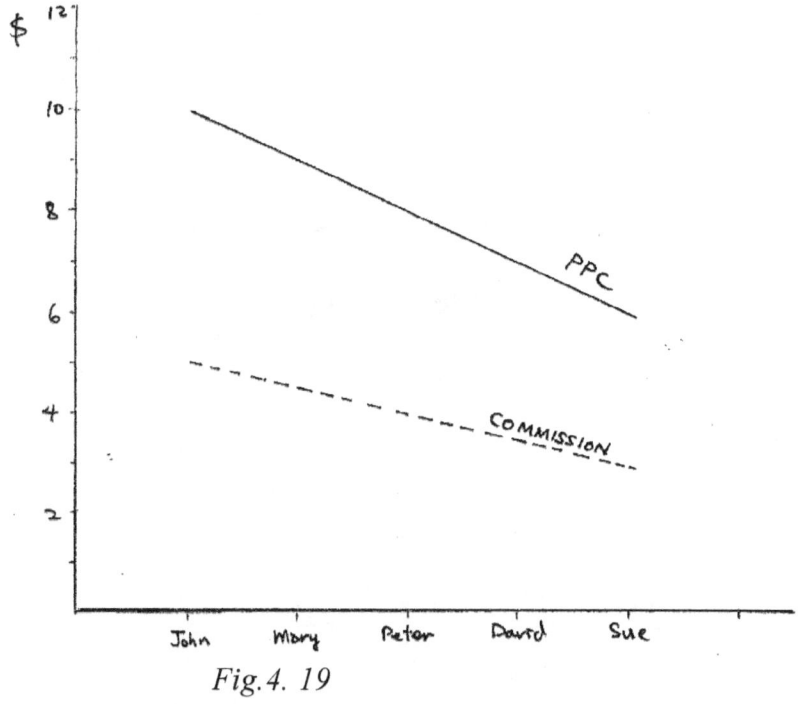

Fig.4. 19

Since employees work at PPC level with 50 percent commission, John will get $5.00, Mary will get $4.50, Peter will get $4.00, David will get $3.50, and Sue will get $3.00. And the company will have economic rent at $20.00 per hour ($5+$4.5+$4+$3.5+$3).

However, the effect of profit sharing depends on the employees' commission rate. If the compensation is $5.00 per hour base wage with only 5 percent after the base wage, that means John will only earn $5.50 per hour if he works wholeheartedly ($5 + ($10 x 5%)). He can earn $5.00 per hour if he only provides $5.00 per hour service. Why does he still work that much harder ($5.00 per hour extra harder) for only $0.50 extra per hour? See figure 4.20.

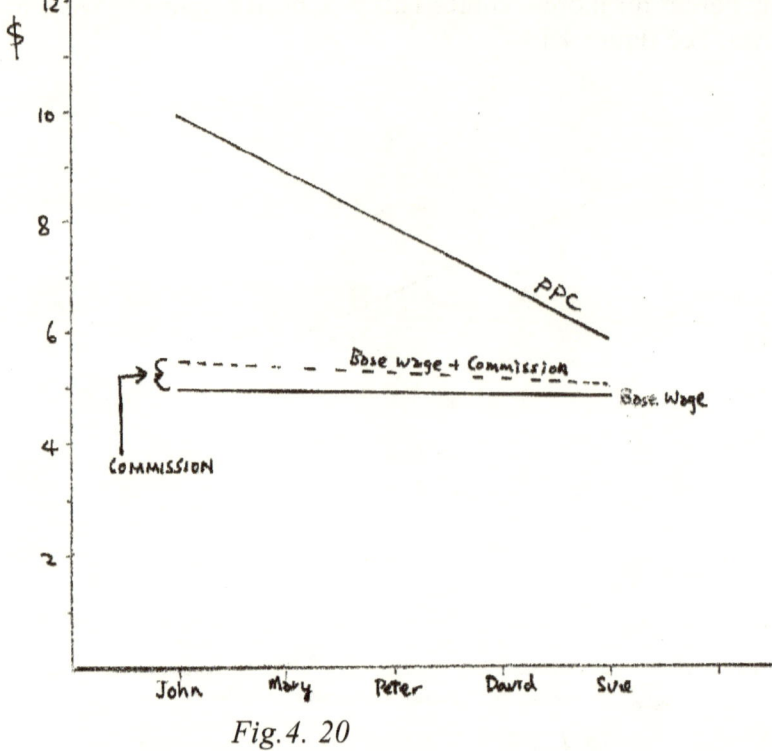

Fig.4. 20

11. Team manager

This may be a new concept of employment nowadays. I believe it will be popular in the future. In a small company, an employer may handle everything from product development, human resources, and even the clerk's job sometimes. When the company is big enough, the owner should consider dividing the labor, even the job of management. The owner will only care about business development and will hire managers to manage different parts of the work.

The owner can use the auction method, the contract method, or the headhunter method to employ a manager and compensate him for doing certain agreed upon jobs. In other words, if the manager can finish his job without hiring any people to help him, he gets all the money.

For example, a big fast-food giant has opened a branch in location Z that is the branch that we used as an example before.

The owner can spend $45.00 per hour on hiring the branch manager based on the budget he has for the business at Branch Z. The agreement will state that the manager will provide $50.00 per hour income to the headquarters from his management services with the compensation of $45.00 per hour.

At Branch Z, the manager, Tim, is appointed by the owner. Tim hired those five employees we mentioned before. See figure 4.21.

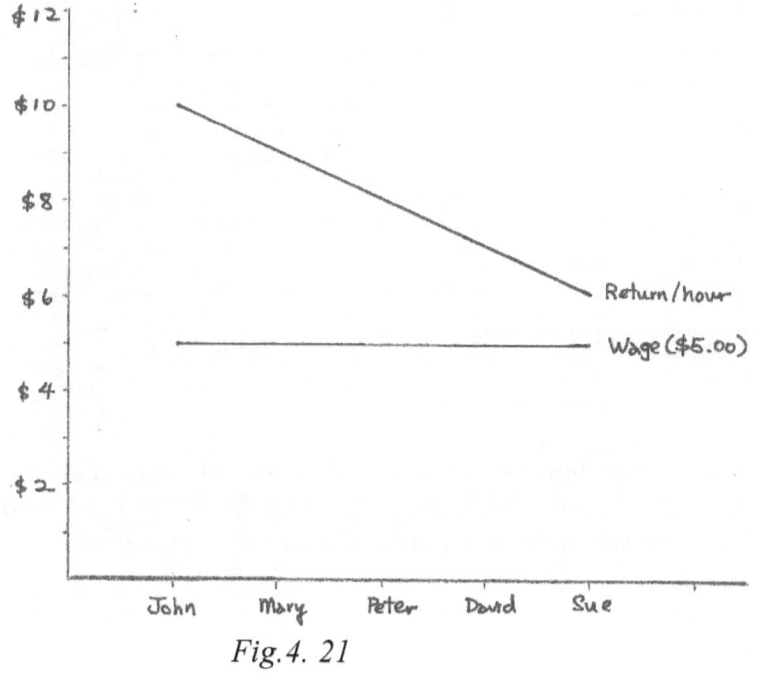

Fig.4. 21

If all employees work at their PPCs, the total return from Branch Z will be $40.00 ($10+$9+$8+$7+$6). That means Tim has failed his mission. So he has to find some way to solve the problem.

Then he hires Joan with a PPC of $11.00 per hour and wage level of $5.00 per hour. Without the diminishing marginal productivity, the total return from Branch Z will be $51.00 per hour. See figure 4.22.

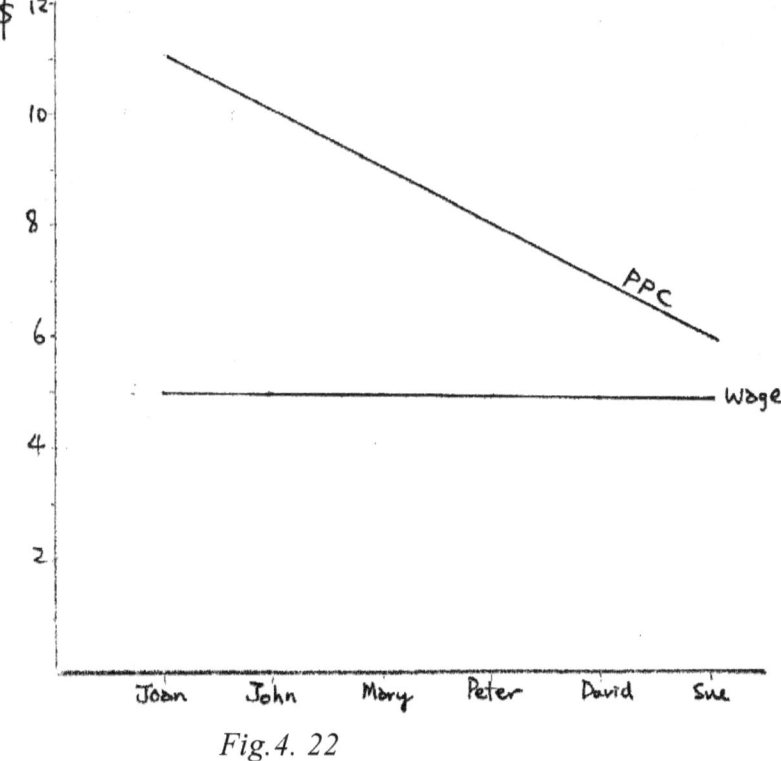

Fig. 4. 22

To the owner, the cost for Branch Z is $45.00 per hour with a return of $51.00 per hour, which means he earns $6.00 per hour from Branch Z. And he will have better control over the budget of his business.

To Tim, the manager at Branch Z, the cost is $30.00 per hour ($5 x 6), and the compensation from the owner is $45.00 as stated in agreement. Tim has a profit of $15.00 per hour.

To all the employees at Branch Z, they all get compensation of $5.00 per hour.

With this result, everybody is happy.

I think this model will be increasingly popular because it is more efficient to hire an employee when an owner has better knowledge of an employee's PPC. The owner actually is not just hiring Tim; the owner is hiring a whole team of Tims, which includes Tim and all the people Tim hired. Before the agreement between the owner and Tim, Tim may have already known all the people he is going to hire. That means he may have a better idea of the PPC of each of these employees. (The longer the history of cooperation between the employees and Tim, the better idea he will have about everyone's PPCs) So the whole company does not need to spend more money on searching for better employees to fit in the position. The owner only has to mind his own business. He does not even need to worry about the risk of hiring the right person for the right job. The risk shifts to the manager, and the manager does his job to make the risk smaller to get more income into his pocket. That is a kind of "division of labor."

That is not all. There are a lot of examples in the world. When you have a question about it, try using PPC theory to explain it.

Chapter 5

Paradox of Exploitation

In the fast-food restaurant example, John works for $10.00 per hour and gets a wage of $5.00 per hour. Is the $5.00 difference ($10.00 - $5.00) exploitation? No, it is not, because $10.00 is John's PPC level. He may not provide service at this level. He could shirk and work as Sue does or even lower to a level equivalent to the $5.00 per hour he makes. In this situation, there will be no difference.

However, the company will have no profit when the return of employees is equal to their wage. The company will not survive. Therefore, employees must work for more than they earn. You may think of it this way: John earns $5.00 per hour. If John does not give up $5.00 ($10.00 - $5.00) to the company, he cannot earn his $5.00 wage. John can think of the $5.00 that goes to the company as rent for all the equipment, the building, the brand name of the restaurant, and so on. That is also the reason why economists call a company's profit "economic rent."

The question is: Why does John need to pay $5.00 rent for his $5.00 wage while Sue can just pay $1.00 rent for her $5.00 wage? It seems unfair. Well, actually, no one will or can tell you what their PPC levels on a specific job are. Bosses and employers have to have some ways to find that out and keep them working their APCs close to their PPC levels to earn the maximum profit.

Bosses and employers do their jobs to make employees work harder, so employers can get their profit or economic rent from the employees' hard work.

What is Exploitation?

To answer this question, we must know the definition of "exploitation" first. So, what is exploitation? I did an Internet search and found this definition on *Wikipedia* (http://en.wikipedia.org): "The act of using another person's labor without offering them an adequate compensation."

According to the definition, John works in a restaurant with a return of $10.00 per hour to the employer for only a $5.00 per hour wage. It seems to be exploitation. However, modern economists may ask why doesn't John just leave his job if he feels exploited? Well! That is true. John is just paying the rent for his $5.00 income. If he feels the $5.00 is too expensive, he can choose another company to work for.

I think the definition of exploitation is still correct, but the main point is on the word "adequate." What is adequate? Adequate means "enough." That implies the employee is willing to work at the level of enough compensation. However, the word "adequate" is subjective. It is different for different people. A subjective concept means you can say you like apples more than you like oranges, but you cannot tell how much more you like between apples and oranges. And also, you cannot say you like apples more than I like apples because your standard is different from mine.

A long time ago, child labor was legal because there were no laws to make it illegal. When people started rethinking the standard, the United States enacted a law that stated only a certain level of child labor was legal because people thought we should not exploit children but educate them. Compared to other countries where people are still living in hunger, how could they consider education without first feeding their tummies? If they made child labor illegal in those countries, people would think that was exploiting the survival rights of children. In this example, we may find a point: if most people think there is exploitation, we would make a law to avoid it.

What about a situation that is not what most people think about? For example, is the length of lunchtime a half hour or one hour? We never made a law about it. That is because people have different opinions about it. However, employees can still make agreements with their employer on the topic. That is called a contract or an agreement.

A law is a contract with nationwide acceptance. An employee handbook is a contract within a company. An employment agreement is a contract between the individual employee and the employer.

If John thinks he has been exploited because his lunchtime is too short, he can request a longer one in the agreement. Everything in the agreement represents adequate compensation for him to work for the company.

A contract goes two ways. While the employee can request how much the "adequate" compensation is in the contract, the employer can also request how much return the employee should provide under the agreed compensation. In other words, the employer can also set a level of productivity in the agreement. John may say he agrees to return $7.00 to $8.00 per hour to the company when the company provides him $5.00 per hour wages with one hour lunchtime every day and a work schedule from 9:00 a.m. to 5:00 p.m., Monday through Friday. Then the company will have control over its economic rent, and John will get enough compensation for providing his services to the company. Everything outside the contract can be treated as exploitation. The employer cannot force the employee to work on Sunday after the contract is signed, or that is exploitation.

If necessary, both sides can amend the agreement. Let's say John adds the statement, "Working on Sunday is counted as overtime, and the company needs to pay 50 percent extra for each hour." If both sides agree, a new agreement is formed. Therefore, the more detail in the agreement, the more protection for both sides of employment.

Examples for discussion:
In wartime, some captives are forced to work building defense structures. These people are forced to work on a job to provide profit, of course, without being offered an adequate compensation. If captives do not work, they may be executed. Is that exploitation? Under the standard of the United Nations, this is exploitation. But the captives may not think that way at that moment since the compensation is living without being killed. Is that enough compensation?

In some countries, it is arranged for people to work in country-owned organizations no matter what they are good at. The United States would say that is exploitation. These countries would say that is their law, so it is not exploitation. Moreover, as I have observed, people working in country-owned organization do not seem to be exploited. From the 1970s to 1980s, China was one of these countries. The government arranged for people to work in different country-owned organizations. Their wages were the same at RMB$36.00. No matter if they worked hard or not. Therefore, people would be as lazy as they could be. It became the figure 5.1 situation.

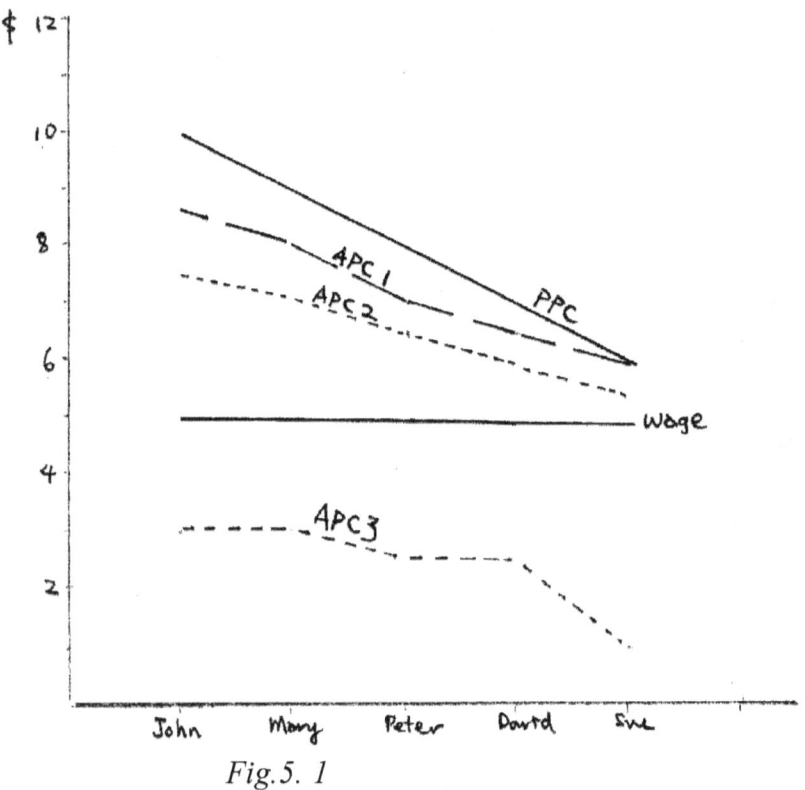

Fig.5. 1

The country-owned organization could not have any profit at all or even loss. The APC would have decreased from APC1 to APC2 or even to APC3. As a result, I don't think that it was exploitation in that case. But you may argue that the people's right to freedom was exploited. Yes, that is correct based on the United States' standard, but not on the Chinese standard at that moment because there was no law about freedom of choice, or the concept of freedom was different in the country at that time.

So, what about a prisoner working in prison? Well! It may or may not be exploitation. Prisoners are forced to work in some states or countries. From a legal perspective, even in the United States they have been exploited because they lost their rights to freedom as punishment. The law says that and it is not wrong. The law also states that after they finish their punishment, they will be free again. So in the long run, they are not exploited at all.

How about volunteers? I have no doubt about saying that it is not exploitation. First, there is no one forcing volunteers to work. Moreover, the reputation or happiness they receive from helping people is priceless. That means the return of being a volunteer is so very high that no money can even count it, and volunteers are working at their own will.

Chapter 6

Unions

Under the National Labor Relations Act in the United States, an election is held to choose a collective bargaining agent for a union. The agent that wins a majority of the votes becomes the exclusive bargaining agent for all workers in the collective bargaining unit. Once a collective bargaining agent has been officially certified, a firm can only bargain with the bargaining agent, so that chiseling is effectively made illegal. No single worker can work additional hours by accepting a lower hourly wage, nor can any outsider come in by offering to work for less.

Unions have their own definition for their existence. In PPC theory, all unions have the same goal: to even up the PPCs of employees, and to keep anyone in the job under the unions' protection.

1. Change the status from wage taker to wage giver
   If the job is not very specific to a special field, there may be a lot of people to compete for the job. Like a cashier in a fast-food restaurant. Employees do not need to have special skills. Almost everyone is qualified for that job. As a result, employees are willing to accept lower wages to get the job. If you don't accept the lower wage the company offers, you may lose the job. The more competitors for the job, the more likely they are to lose their bargaining power over wages and become wage takers.

The union tries to turn the table. They bargain for the wages of all employees. If the company refuses their request, they strike. It is like they set an all-or-nothing price for the employer. The company takes the option or no employee will be able to work for the company. The law states that the company can only negotiate with the union agent. If a union has been formed, the company cannot hire anyone who is not a union member or not protected by the union. Therefore, the union balances the power of bargaining for wages.

2. All employees are protected
   Not all employees have the same PPC. See figure 6.1.

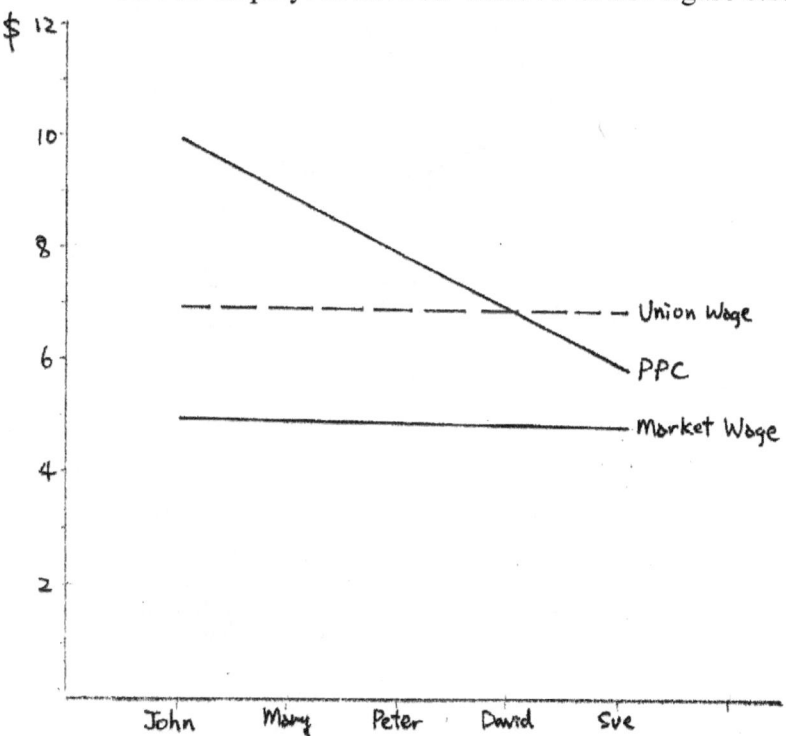

Fig.6. 1

The union wage must be higher than the market wage; that is why the union is there. When the union bargained for the wage with the company at $8.00, Sue's PPC was lower than the union wage level. If Sue was a union member, she was protected, and the company could not fire her. The $1.00 per hour loss from hiring Sue will be deducted from the economic rent area by the company.

However, John may shirk and work just like Sue since Sue works for less return but was still hired. Eventually, the company will experience a huge loss and may go out of business. See figure 6.2.

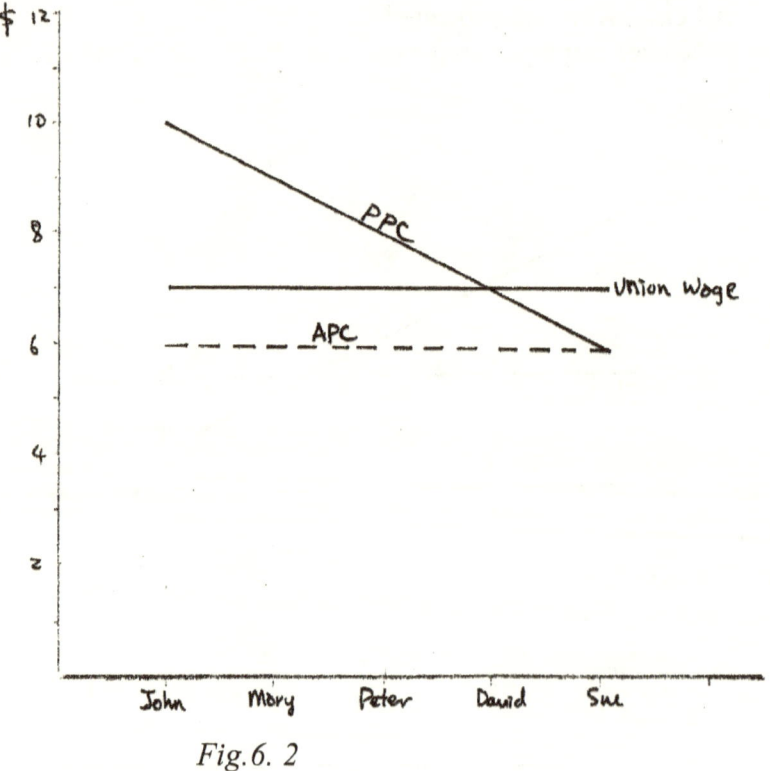

Fig.6. 2

To avoid all of the company's economic rent vanishing, the employer has to find some way to push up the APC.

3. Pursue better benefits

As you can see from the example in point 2 in this chapter, if the wage is set too high, the company will loss economic rent. But that does not always happen. In most cases, the union wage is set at a low-level, so point 2 will not happen yet. Since the wage was not set high enough for the employees, the union may bargain for more benefits for members. Like a maximum work hour, for example. The union can set a unified agreement with better benefits for all members and negotiate with the company. With the agreement between the union and the company, things, hopefully, will be better for both parties and become a win-win situation. With the union's power, every minority employee will become a big voice and form a majority power. Since the union can bargain for more benefits in the employment agreement that also means exploitation can be minimized.

4. Political power

Every year Congress discusses the budget for our country. They make decisions about taxation and how to distribute the tax money too. Some countries have their union party or labor party to represent all the labors. So the government can make more decisions that lean on the side of labor. Earned income credit (EIC) is a refundable credit that helps all working people who are low income to improve their living standard. If we don't have union power in government, all benefits will go to other areas, such as a credit for a first house purchase, for example, which is not related to the labor class at all.

The larger the union, the more votes can be used for the labor class.

Conclusion

Potential performance curve is a brand-new concept for looking at the factor market in economics. It is not used to refute the theory of marginal productivity. As you can see in this book, I still recommend that all of you examine marginal productivity in more detail in other books. Indeed, marginal productivity is a very useful theory for explaining the factor market.

I did not say PPC is less powerful than marginal productivity, either. You may say they are two different ways to see the same thing. Claiming one is more powerful or more accurate for explaining human behavior is not my point. I created this theory and wrote this book because I wanted to provide a whole new way for all of you to review the real world.

After you read this entire book, you will have a better idea of what we are actually dealing with in the workplace every day. Everything is happening for a reason. The workplace is not really a battlefield. With a proper company policy, management direction, and all rational employees' considered, we all could be working in a win-win situation. Everything is just about the math.

I have said enough. It is your turn to think about it.

World peace!

Notes

www.ingramcontent.com/pod-product-compliance
Lightning Source LLC
Chambersburg PA
CBHW021023180526
45163CB00005B/2079